Garage, Attic & Basement STORAGE

By the Editors of Sunset Books and Sunset Magazine

LANE PUBLISHING CO. • Menlo Park, California

We wish to thank the architects, designers, and homeowners whose innovative ideas for storage are included in this book. A special thank-you goes to Kirsten Fedderke for her assistance in assembling the color section.

Cover: Boxes, baskets, bins, shelves . . . these are tools of the storage trade. Labels and see-through panels make them especially convenient; pegboard, hooks, and brackets make them adaptable. Photographed by Jack McDowell. Cover design by Zan Fox.

Photographers

Gerald Fredrick: 28. **Gene Hamilton:** 36, 60 left, 62. **Jack McDowell:** 3, 4, 5 top and bottom left, 11, 12, 13 bottom, 14, 19, 20, 21 left, 22, 29 left, 35, 37, 38, 43, 44, 45 top, 46, 51, 53, 59, 60 right, 61. **Steve W. Marley:** 5 bottom right, 27 left, 30. **Ells Marugg:** 29 right. **Rob Super:** 45 bottom left. **Tom Wyatt:** 6, 13 top, 21 right, 27 right, 54.

Editor, Sunset Books:
David E. Clark

First printing October 1982

Supervising Editor:
Maureen Williams Zimmerman

Staff Editors: **Susan E. Schlangen**

Susan Warton

Contributing Editor: **Scott Atkinson**

Design: **Roger Flanagan**

Photo Editor: **JoAnn Masaoka Lewis**

Illustrations: **Rik Olson**

Contents

Behind sturdy blonde doors, *this custom storage wall works hard at organizing a garage-load of goods. Architect: Glenn D. Brewer.*

About This Book...

Some of life's greatest pleasures are associated with the possessions we own and must store—garden tools that help ensure fragrant blossoms in spring, sleek new skis that sink into fresh powdery snow, sturdy old suitcases that wear the scars of travel as surely as we carry the memories. It seems that the more we enjoy life, the more we have to store.

What's *your* storage situation? Do you know where you'll stack the firewood to stoke the new wood stove you've been thinking about? How will you put to use the knowledge gained at that great wine class, if you don't have a proper place to store wine? What do you do with your multiplying financial records, mystery novels, family photos?

We think it's best to start simply. That's why our first section (pages 6–11) is devoted to storage units and accessories. You'll be pleased at how much even a few hooks, racks, and bins can do. For specific belongings, we've included an item-by-item storage section (pages 12–59). Filled with ideas, it's an alphabetical showcase that tells you what to do with items—outdoor furniture, sports equipment, and workshop supplies—that may be stumbling blocks in your storage path. The section also contains special features about auxiliary storage areas—the patio, deck, and garden shed—and a feature on storage safety.

Crowded garages, stuffy attics, and wet basements receive in-depth treatment in the back of the book (pages 60–79). Here, we explain ways to remedy some of the more complicated but common problems of garage, attic, and basement storage.

A place for everything and *everything in its place. Pine board and vertical plywood spacers form cubbyholes—large ones for basketballs and ice skates, small ones for wine and miscellany. See pages 8–9 for more shelving ideas.*

Open doors reveal *garbage cans, counter, shelves for supplies, and combination woodbin and pass-through. Architects: The Hastings Group.*

Loft frees floor space *below for table saw, freezer, extra refrigerator. Commercial fold-down stairs offer easy access to lightweight storables. For more on lofts, see page 65.*

"Tools" of the Storage Trade

Pegs, hooks & racks • shelving • boxes & bins • cabinets & closets

Simple storage aids *can handle complex storage needs. Here, a modest shelving unit corrals camping gear and gardening equipment, nails grip tennis rackets, and a bin brims with sports gear. The bike dangles from ceiling hooks.*

It's the hottest day of the year, and you still haven't stored your winter woollies, holiday decorations, and snow tires. Don't worry; you're suffering from a common ailment. And here you'll find some tested remedies—the most basic storage units and accessories.

This section is like a catalogue, with some tips to help you select the kinds of storage units and accessories best suited to your needs. The emphasis is on simple, utilitarian storage aids that are easy to build or install: pegs, hooks, racks, shelves, boxes, bins, cabinets, and closets. Many of these items can be purchased in a variety of colors, materials, and designs.

You'll probably want to choose a combination of open and closed storage. Open storage—for example, heavy-duty hooks securely fastened to garage wall studs—may be ideal for hanging up your snow tires. Fragile holiday decorations, on the other hand, require closed storage—say, cardboard boxes on track and bracket shelves—for protection from dust, moisture, and accidents.

By adding a few storage aids, you'll open up more floor space and gain better clearance—important benefits in full garages, attics with steep walls, and basements. You may even discover new space for work or play.

Consult *Sunset's* companion volumes, *Wall Systems & Shelving* and *How to Make Bookshelves & Cabinets*, for more details on tools, techniques, and materials.

Pegs, hooks and racks

Pegs and hooks are the simplest storage aids, great for items that you want immediately accessible. Use them to hang objects from walls, ceiling joists, rafters, shelf undersides, and cabinet interiors. Rack systems, which make use of pegs and hooks, provide great storage diversity and capacity.

Pegs and hooks are particularly easy to install. For pegs, you can use large carpenters' nails hammered into wall studs or rafters, dowels recessed into drilled holes, spring clips, and even cabinet pull knobs hung on the wall. The range of hooks available includes coat hooks in many sizes, shapes, and materials; cup hooks screwed into shelf undersides; and large hooks for hanging such heavy items as bicycles (see page 15).

Wall racks are great for organizing garden tools, outdoor clothing, folding lawn chairs, hand tools, sports equipment, and many other items. The classic rack system for garages is a pegboard equipped with various hooks and hangers. Pegboard, or perforated hardboard, is made in ⅛ and ¼-inch thicknesses; install ¼-inch board for heavy-duty use. When you install pegboard, use spacers to hold it slightly away from the wall, allowing clearance for hooks.

Racks made of steel and vinyl-coated steel have either horizontal or vertical metal tracks or grids that attach to the wall. Both kinds can be equipped with a range of accessories—from hooks to shelf brackets to hanging bins—to handle specific storables.

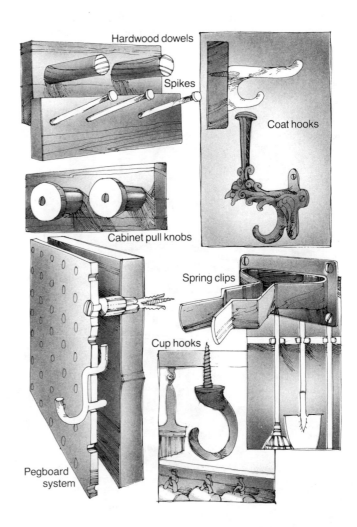

Hardwood dowels

Spikes

Coat hooks

Cabinet pull knobs

Spring clips

Cup hooks

Pegboard system

Shelves

Shelves and storage go hand in hand...the two words are almost synonymous. Shelves can be hung from the wall, suspended from the ceiling or rafters, or used to span an enclosed frame or opposing walls. Adjustable shelves and freestanding shelf units give you more flexibility, but are less stable for heavy loads.

Formal shelving units are unnecessary in storage areas. Instead, consider the following simple, less expensive ways to assemble basic units or fasten individual shelves to walls or ceilings.

Materials. What materials make good shelves for storage? Sturdy utilitarian shelves can be made from solid fir or pine, plywood, or particle board. Fir is stronger than pine, but pine is less expensive. Plywood is best for shelves more than 12 inches deep. Larger platforms can be fashioned from hollow-core doors or plywood and supported by a solid lumber frame (see page 65). You can cut your own shelves, ask lumberyard personnel to cut them for you, or purchase precut or preassembled units. Easy-to-clean plastic laminate shelves are handy for laundry or crafts areas.

Shelf spans. When planning your shelving, follow this rule: no shelf should have a span of more than 48 inches. For light loads, 1-inch thick lumber spanning 32 inches is ideal; for medium to heavy loads, shorten the span to 24 or even 16 inches, or use 2-inch-thick lumber. For very strong shelves, sandwich together two layers of ¾-inch plywood with glue, and reinforce with 1 by 2-inch strips around the edges (see drawing below). Heavy particle board shelves tend to sag, regardless of the load; if you use particle board, keep the spans very short.

Blocks and boards. Stack bricks or cinder blocks to support solid lumber or plywood shelves, preferably against a wall. If your stack is higher than 5 feet, anchor the top shelf to the wall.

Brackets. Common shelf brackets (with or without gusset supporters), continuous Z-brackets, or L-braces are easiest for fastening individual shelves or a small series of shelves to the wall.

Cleats and ledgers. Made from 1 by 2 trim or L-shaped aluminum molding, cleats and ledgers can be used to support shelves that span opposing walls and rafters or the insides of closets and cabinets. Cleats hold up the shelf ends, and a ledger runs along the back edge (see drawing below). For extra support, use 2 by 4s.

Ropes and chains. Suspended from eyescrews attached to ceiling joists or rafters, ropes and chains provide sturdy shelf support. Rope is knotted—or clamped with electrical cable clamps (see drawing below)—to secure shelves. Chain-supported shelves

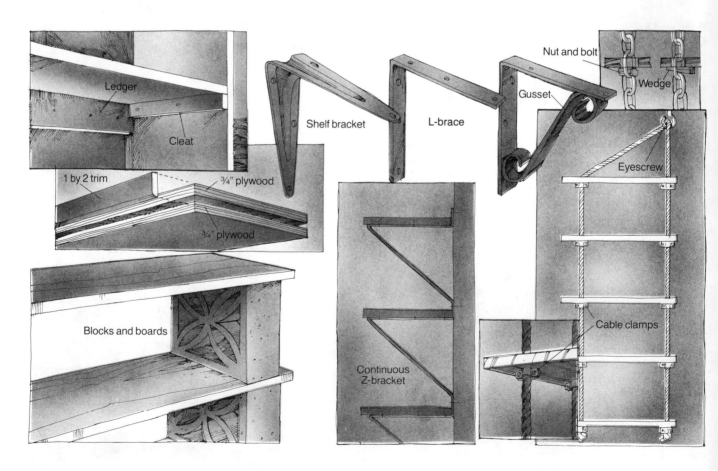

Ledger

Cleat

1 by 2 trim

¾" plywood

¾" plywood

Blocks and boards

Shelf bracket

L-brace

Continuous Z-bracket

Nut and bolt

Wedge

Gusset

Eyescrew

Cable clamps

must be wedged in place with wood scraps or secured with nuts, bolts, and washers below each shelf. Attach chains to the eyescrews with S-hooks. For added stability, also attach the ends of the ropes or chains to the wall behind.

Ladder supports. Use old ladders or build them from 2 by 2 or larger lumber. Suspend them from ceiling joists or rafters, or tie them together with cross braces for a freestanding unit. Nailing shelves in place will help stabilize the unit.

Adjustable shelving hardware. Track systems—tracks and brackets, or tracks and clips—have become the most popular way to hang a series of adjustable shelves. Generally, bracket systems are hung on a wall, and clips are used within a cabinet frame or other enclosed area. Brackets are available in several styles and finishes; the most common sizes accommodate 8, 10, or 12-inch-deep shelves, but some systems will support shelves up to 24 inches deep. For heavy loads, use industrial systems. Adjustable clips are made in two designs: gusseted and flush (see drawing below). The gusseted type holds more weight.

Tracks should be fastened to wall studs if possible, especially if your shelves will bear a lot of weight. If you must fasten tracks to wall coverings alone, you'll need spreading anchors or toggle bolts for the job. If your walls are block, brick, or solid concrete, you'll have to use masonry fasteners (see pages 78–79).

Boxes and bins

Midway between shelving and more formal cabinetry are boxes and bins—containers more casual than cabinets, more protective than shelves.

Bins: tilt-outs and roll-outs. The most useful storage bins tilt or roll out from beneath a counter, from inside a cabinet or closet, or from along a room's perimeter. They're excellent space savers. Roll-out bins are good for moving items to and from a congested work area; tilt-outs angle down for quick top access.

Boxes: build, buy, or recycle. When stacked with some kind of support, cardboard boxes and wood crates don't clutter up the floor or fall apart. Try organizing them on wide shelves, or on a frame made as shown below.

Wood boxes can be hung from wall studs with nails or screws, or attached to a piece of plywood.

Box modules. A set of box modules consists of plywood boxes that you construct. They fit together well because they're all alike or have complementary dimensions. Rectangular units (see drawing below) should be exactly twice as long as square modules.

Build modules from ¾-inch exterior plywood, then finish them with enamel or polyurethane. Bolt high stacks together or bolt them to the wall. Add simple doors or pull-out drawers for a fancy system.

"Ladder" supports

Tracks and clips

Flush

Gusseted

Tracks and brackets

Standard

Heavy-duty

Adjustable

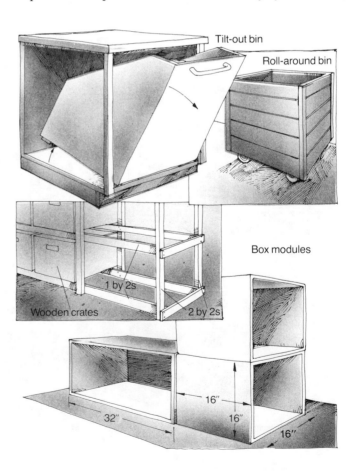

Tilt-out bin

Roll-around bin

Box modules

1 by 2s

2 by 2s

Wooden crates

32"

16"

16"

16"

Cabinets, closets, or both?

Cabinets and closets rank above other kinds of storage units in usefulness, complexity, organization, and cost. Efficient cabinets and closets—whether freestanding, framed in, or hung from a wall or ceiling—often include other storage components such as shelves, drawers, rods, and hooks. For ultimate flexibility, an integrated storage wall of both cabinets and closets is ideal. Consider the following features when shopping for premade units or when building or refurbishing closets and cabinets for the garage or basement.

Doors. You have several choices: hinged, sliding, folding, and roll-up. A hinged door—whether of the flush, lip, or overhanging type—gives you quick access to what's inside; it's also the most secure and weathertight kind of door. However, hinged doors on large units may be heavy and unwieldy, and hinged doors require more clearance than other kinds of doors. Sliding doors—with wood, metal, or plastic tracks—demand no clearance, but allow access to only half of a closet or cabinet at any one time. Bifold doors are a good compromise for large units; they're usually louvered, which allows for ventilation. Roll-ups of plastic or canvas are economical choices, but not as durable or protective.

Drawers. Odds and ends that have a way of getting lost need drawers. Ideally, drawers should be no deeper than 30 inches and no taller than 12 inches.

You can build your own drawers—a sticky task for the uninitiated—or choose from a large selection of manufactured drawers or "drawer frames" (drawers, hardware, and the support frame). Before building or buying, select your drawer guides. Commercially made guides are usually the smoothest. However, simpler systems of wooden strips or plastic channels work adequately for most loads. Lightweight drawers that won't carry much weight can slide in and out without guides.

The case for closets. Large, open closets are effective for storing seasonal clothing, garden and house maintenance goods, cleaning supplies, firewood—even roll-out bins and power tools on casters. Design your closet for many uses: add clothes rods, hooks, or pegboard walls inside; shelves or cabinets above; and a bank of drawers. This kind of unit is especially useful if security is a problem; the outer doors can be locked.

Security and safety. Depending on the contents and location of your cabinet or closet, you may want to make it secure. To foil burglars, use a heavy-duty padlock with a steel or solid brass case and a hardened steel shackle attached to an integral bolt and security hasp. When closed, the hasp should cover the screws that attach it to the unit. If you're worried about keeping your children out, a simpler, less expensive lock and hasp should do. Purchase rust-resistant locks, bolts, and hasps. Standard hinged doors, especially with hinges mounted to the inside of the unit, offer the most protection.

Hinged door

Sliding door

Roll-up door

Commercial drawer runners

Bifold door

To 30"

To 12"

Security hasp

Padlock

Storage bays. *To gain storage space without crowding cars, bays were built in three walls of this new garage. Each projection hangs from the rafters and features narrow side windows. Two include plywood shelves on a frame built of 1 by 4s; the third has a workbench instead of shelves. The projection in the side wall shown at right takes advantage of an underused side yard. A similar bay can be added to an existing garage as part of a remodeling project.*

Item-by-Item Storage Ideas

From bicycles and books to workshop tools and wines

Reels on redwood door. *Fishing reels and fishing line hang on the inside of a redwood door. Items are placed so the door closes without disturbing tackle boxes and other gear on shelves. Design: Jean Chappell.*

All in a line. *Everything has its place on this brightly painted garage wall. Tools, some of which dangle from cords looped through holes drilled in the handles, hang on nails. Fuel is stored in safety cans.*

Sideways rungs: a storage switch. *Simple wooden racks, securely attached to the garage beams and positioned for convenience and clearance, support an extra-long ladder. Cars are removed when ladder is being loaded and unloaded. Design: Emil Marent.*

Bicycle Bulk

Space-saving ways to keep bikes off the floor, out of harm's way

If your family has caught the cycling bug, you've no doubt discovered that those bikes take up a lot of space. To accommodate bicycles, you can add an extension to your garage (see below), make do with available parking space, or look for another likely storage spot around the house or yard.

In the garage, get lightweight 10-speed bikes off the ground if possible. You'll save floor space and probably boost the life of your tires, which tend to crack and go flat when left sitting on the floor over

long periods of time. A solid bike rack or hook can be especially handy at repair time: while the rack holds the bike in place, your hands are free to do the work. Heavier bikes should be stored on floor stands such as the ones shown in the drawing on the facing page.

No garage? If you have to store bikes in a carport, security can be a problem. Lockable, walk-in closet units are one way to guard against both theft and weather. A patio or garden shed can also provide shelter for your bikes.

Angle parking without a scratch

A bicycle shed in a garage? Sure! This 3 by 16-foot extension provides enough space to angle-park a family of bikes—and even wheel them in or out alongside a parked car. Pushed-out garage side wall and extended foundation made it all possible; a shingled roof and matching redwood siding nailed to studs completed the project. New side wall is ideal for hanging storage, and alcove at end keeps wood scraps in order.

Clever hang-ups

Brightly colored screw hooks from the cycling shop, driven into wall studs or ceiling joists, support bicycles with ease. More elegant braced wall brackets—originally intended for a closet rod—give better clearance from the wall (secure them solidly with ¼ by 3-inch screws). Stagger single hooks to hang several bikes close together; two brackets secure both wheels of a bike high above the floor.

Hoist them high

This handsome, easy-to-build rack made from fir 2 by 4s and 1 by 3s keeps bicycles off the floor and out of the way. Notches in each upright board slip over a ceiling joist and are secured with 4-inch carriage bolts; lap joint notches at the opposite ends cradle the 1 by 3 racks. Adjust the diagram dimensions to fit your bikes, the garage height, and the height of cars beneath.

Stand them, school-style

Bicycle floor stands—like those from the school playground —are very convenient at home. Buy commercial racks or build your own from L-shaped slotted metal channel and nuts and bolts from hardware stores. Or check with local building suppliers for cement bike blocks that have slots for front bicycle wheels. Though heavy enough to stay put when you want, bike blocks can still be moved as needs and seasons change.

Books, Documents & Photographs

Pamper paper—it damages easily

Books, magazines, personal documents, financial records, photographs, and correspondence: no collection grows faster, is more difficult to keep organized, and requires such stable storage conditions. Light, moisture, heat, insects, and poor ventilation are all enemies of stored paper products.

What conditions are ideal? Librarians recommend temperatures between 60 and 75° and humidity between 50 and 60 percent for storing most papers. If you use good quality storage units that permit air circulation, a dry and insulated attic or basement should be fine. For photographs and papers that need to be perfectly preserved, hot attics and damp basements are out (see pages 68–73 and 74–79 for more details and solutions).

If you store paper items in cardboard boxes, the lids or flaps should be loose enough to allow a free flow of air. Pack books and magazines loosely, and check occasionally for signs of dampness or mold. Metal units or units lined with metal (see drawing on page 75) will protect paper from insects and rodents. Boxes—whether of cardboard or metal—block out light, as well.

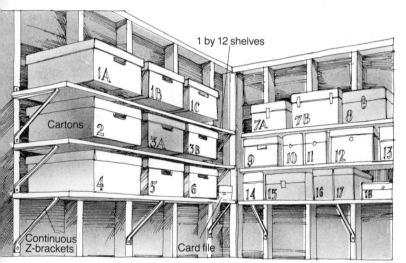

1 by 12 shelves

Cartons

Continuous Z-brackets

Card file

Orderly filing for easier finding

An organized collection of cardboard or metal containers for household records, receipts, documents, and correspondence will meet the storage needs of most homeowners.

Individual filing boxes or cartons handle large items. Also available are canceled check organizers with filing inserts, slipcover letter files, and binding cases for documents. Metal and cardboard card files—manufactured in many sizes—make compact containers for lots of bits and pieces of paper.

Arrange your box system on 1 by 12-inch shelves supported by continuous Z-brackets or individual shelf brackets. To keep track of what's where, number each box to match a corresponding index card listing the contents of the box.

Space-saving file cabinets: Safe as houses, almost as strong

A metal office file cabinet, with one to five stacked drawers, is a very efficient and safe way to store important documents and photo negatives. If appearance and neatness count, recess the file cabinet into a knee wall or under stairs, for example, so that only the drawer fronts are exposed. For maps, oversize documents, and art paper, use wood or steel flat files. File cabinets are expensive, but you can reduce the cost by purchasing used equipment; look up "Office Furniture and Equipment—Used" in the Yellow Pages.

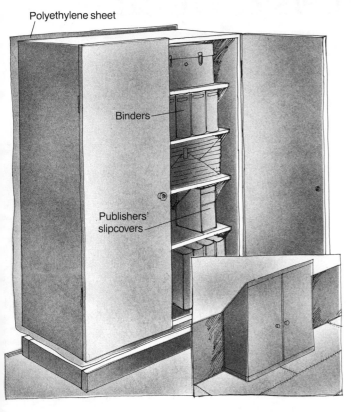

Polyethylene sheet

Binders

Publishers' slipcovers

Catching library overflow

Lovers of the printed word are always running out of shelf space for their collections of mysteries, reference texts, or favorite magazines. Inevitably, part of the library is "off to storage."

Even in the attic or basement, books and magazines should be stored on standard shelves. Set up shelves in a dry area that has a stable temperature. It's all right to store books in a cold area as long as it's dry. Don't place shelves against a wall that hasn't been insulated; fur out the wall (see page 78) or at least place polyethylene sheeting between the wall and shelves. If your books will be exposed to a lot of light, especially direct daylight or fluorescent light, the shelves should be equipped with doors or curtains. Magazines can be stored in slipcover cases or binders sold by publishers or office suppliers.

Protecting photos & film

Fortunately, photographic films and papers are more stable and long-lasting today than they were in the past, but your photo memories can still fade or discolor if exposed to excessive light, heat, or moisture. Keep them in covered boxes, cupboards, or flat file drawers. Place a small amount of silica gel in each container to help absorb moisture. Storage conditions for photo materials must be temperate and dry.

Store color transparencies in boxed projector trays or special clear plastic 8½ by 11-inch sheets. Black and white and color negatives are best kept in negative file sheets inside a binder and drawer. Separate prints with pieces of paper or enclose them in individual rag paper envelopes, and lay them in flat file drawers or boxes.

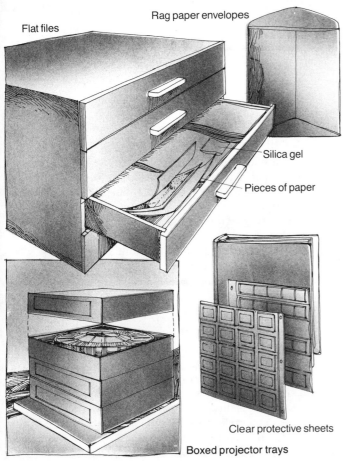

Flat files

Rag paper envelopes

Silica gel

Pieces of paper

Clear protective sheets

Boxed projector trays

Cans, Glass, Newspapers & Discards

Simple sorting systems for home recycling and disposal

Taking out the garbage is a familiar chore, but recycling is a newer responsibility for most of us—and easy enough when you're organized. You'll need up to four adjacent bins for presorting and storing tin, aluminum, glass, and newspaper. An easy-to-carry container located in or near the kitchen will save you extra steps until you have a full load. Bins should be lightweight and made of plastic, metal, or plywood treated for moisture.

Place both garbage cans and recycling bins in any well-ventilated area protected from the elements: a corner just inside the garage door, a carport enclosure, or a small outdoor shelter in the side or back yard (check local building codes before constructing). For convenience, cans and bins shouldn't be too far from either the kitchen or the driveway or street. Prefabricated metal garbage can shelters, whether separate or part of a large garden shed (see pages 42–43), are handy.

Stackable slide-outs save space

Neatly separated recyclables await pickup within a stack of lipped plastic laundry baskets. On recycling days, the baskets easily slide forward and out. A welder assembled the iron brackets shown, but you can attach wooden drawer guides or cleats inside an open cabinet frame to hold each basket. Or for a more finished look, try one of the commercial bin systems that roll on their own frames.

Plastic laundry basket

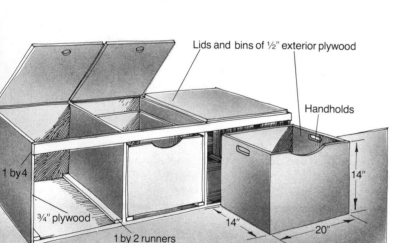

Lids and bins of ½" exterior plywood

Handholds

1 by 4

¾" plywood

1 by 2 runners

14"

14"

20"

Sorting bins swallow plenty

Here's a basic enclosed three-bin recycling system; you can modify it for special needs. Side-by-side bins house recyclable aluminum, tin, and glass. (You might install an extra large newspaper bin, too—papers pile up quickly.) You can leave the hinged tops up for easy access, or flip them down to double as counter space. On recycling days, slide each bin out by gripping the cutout on the front, then carry by using the two side handholds.

Don't lug it. Roll it.

Do you dread the weekly chore of lugging heavy overflowing garbage cans out to the curb and back? A simple remedy is to mobilize those cans. A crisscross dolly on wheels, sized to fit, is the answer for one can; two cans can ride in style on the rolling wagon shown. Pull the wagon up and down the driveway with a thick rope or chain handle.

A messy subject comes clean

Neat alcove solves several dilemmas: the cans are out of view, yet accessible from inside or outside the garage. On pickup day, the cans can be moved while the main garage doors remain locked. Design: Victoria G. Gilmour.

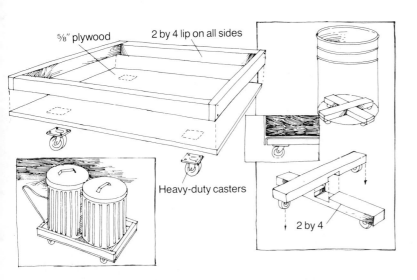

⅝″ plywood

2 by 4 lip on all sides

Heavy-duty casters

2 by 4

Coping with All-weather Wear

How to contain the mess and let outdoor clothing dry

Whether you must deal with snow-caked boots, sandy sneakers, or rain-soaked jackets, a "mudroom" can save both your temper and the garments themselves. In this spot close to an exterior door, clothing can be shed and left to dry.

A mudroom ideally is furnished with a long bench for removing wet boots and rain pants, and pegs or hooks and a long shelf for parkas, gloves, and hats. Equip the area beneath the bench with drawers or a storage chest for dry socks and shoes. Deep, open cubbyhole shelves or a clothes closet and bureau turn an enclosed mudroom into a changing area.

A complete mudroom might include some source of heat—an adjacent water heater or heating duct— to help clothes dry quickly (for a heated shelf idea, see page 47). A louver or pegboard closet door and a ventilating fan inside the closet help check moisture and odor buildup. A floor cover of removable wooden slats or a galvanized metal grate allows water to drip down to a waterproof floor; the grates and slats also allow air circulation. In truly muddy climates, install a faucet and drain for rinsing boots and rain gear.

Concealed pull-down

The space between the joists in this basement makes room for an overhead pull-down compartment, an easily accessible hiding place for ski boots or other gear. Outdoor clothing for rain and cold weather hangs on a metal closet rod just below the pull-down.

Heel toe, heel toe

Shoes and boots hang on dowels recessed at an upward slant into a thick board. The board is bolted to a wall stud. Easy-care flooring makes cleanup simple. A tension closet rod fits neatly below the sloped understair ceiling.

Corner cache catches all

Before entering the house, family members shed their out-door wear in a storage corner in the garage. The clothes rack, built of 1 by 2s that rest on triangular supports, holds slickers and jackets. Boots, shoes, and roller skates tuck into bottom compartments. Shelves above organize less frequently used items, including camping supplies and sports equipment.

Clothing in Hibernation

Simple shelters sequester out-of-season wardrobes

The key to storing clothes is protection—from moisture, dust, and insects. Moisture, in the form of condensation or actual seepage, is best controlled within the entire storage area; see pages 75 and 76–77 for details and remedies. Closed units are best where dust or insects are major concerns. Built-ins are the most functional, but steel wardrobes—even the cardboard wardrobes used by movers—provide serviceable closets. To prevent mildew, closed units should be vented with finely screened openings or, for problem cases, an exhaust fan.

A traditional cedar closet or chest will help deter moths. Remember, though, that while cedar repels moths it does not kill them. Cedar-scented moth-controlling substances—spray and solid—can be used inside garment bags, chests, or closets.

Make sure that clothes are thoroughly cleaned before storing them.

A closet for off-season clothes
Make room in bedroom closets by storing out-of-season and seldom-worn clothing in their own portable closet in the garage. When closed, the door protects clothes from dust and light. There's even room for stowing bulky bags and luggage inside and on top.

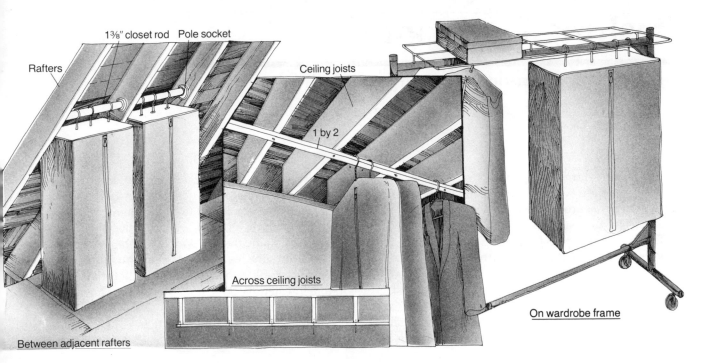

1⅜" closet rod   Pole socket

Rafters

Ceiling joists

1 by 2

Across ceiling joists

On wardrobe frame

Between adjacent rafters

Makeshift closets: quick, easy, safe

Open units are the simplest, though least protected, means to out-of-season clothes storage. Lengths of 1⅜-inch closet rod, adjustable metal rods, or 1 by 2s can be strung between opposing or adjacent attic rafters, fastened to the bottom of ceiling joists, or suspended from chains or ropes. A mobile wardrobe frame is both adjustable and collapsible.

Protect clothes and shoes stored in the open with vinyl or fabric garment bags—available in several types and sizes.

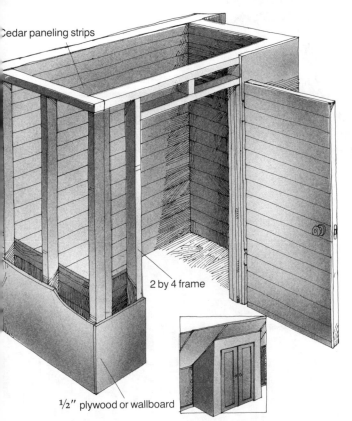

Cedar paneling strips

2 by 4 frame

½" plywood or wallboard

Cedar—for extra care

To fashion your own cedar closet—or to convert an existing closet—line the closet frame inside with tongue-and-groove cedar paneling strips, available in kits from home improvement centers. Just cut the strips to length and lay them in horizontally, one wall at a time, with paneling adhesive and finishing nails. For maximum protection, line the ceiling, floor, and door too. Weatherstrip the door edges tightly.

Don't finish or seal your cedar with varnish—you'll lock the fragrance inside the wood. To revive the fragrance, sand lightly with fine sandpaper.

Stashing Firewood

Protecting wood, seasoning it, getting at it with ease

To an increasing number of people, firewood has become an important supplement or primary alternative to other energy sources which are expensive and sometimes in short supply.

These are basic rules for storing firewood: 1) split the wood before stacking; 2) raise the wood off the ground; and 3) don't pile wood against a house wall—leave some space between the wall and firewood stack.

Wood can be stacked in parallel or perpendicular (crisscross) rows. For safety and neatness, brace tall woodpiles. If you're seasoning wood outside, don't seal it off completely because you'll trap moisture and condensation inside. Instead, store wood under a shed roof in an area sheltered from the elements.

Should you store firewood inside? If you have the space, by all means yes. Wood stored inside dries faster and contains less residual moisture. But before you bring your split wood inside, check it for insects. Don't store infested wood inside. Metal or masonry surfaces below and behind your indoor woodpile will help prevent insects from homesteading in your walls and baseboards.

Snoop around for nooks & crannies

Survey the garage, basement, or carport for likely places to store your firewood. Here are two good places to look: under the basement stairs and below hanging garage or carport cabinets.

Farmhouse idea: the lean-to

This kind of woodshed can be a simple lean-to bin or a full-scale add-on with pass-through access or a door to the house. Keep a simple lean-to open on the sides, and make sure that firewood is raised off the ground. A good roof overhang ensures adequate air circulation and protection from the weather.

Raised off ground

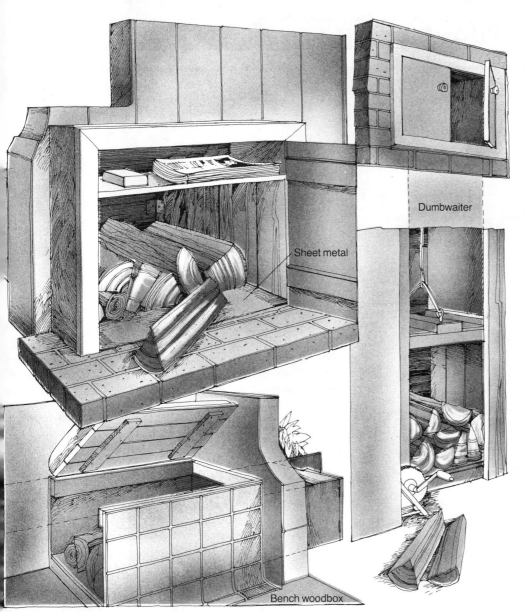

Sheet metal

Dumbwaiter

Bench woodbox

Save toil with pass-through

With a woodpile and a fireplace, the shortest distance between two points is a straight line—that's the idea behind pass-through access doors. If your storage area or add-on woodshed is adjacent to a wall near the fireplace or woodstove, a simple wood box with an interior access door can save you from stepping into the teeth of a gale to stoke the fire on a stormy night. Building codes require that a wood box opening into a garage or carport have a solid-core, self-closing door. To keep insects out of living quarters, line the wood box with sheet metal.

For a stylish variation, store your wood under a fireside bench seat that can be loaded from the outside; when you need a log, just lift the hinged seat. Have a mechanical bent? A basement-to-fireplace dumbwaiter, operated by cables and a hand winch, is a helpful friend to the fire tender.

Solar seasoning

With this unit, green wood is seasoned in far less time than in the open air. The design can be modified to suit your budget, available space, and architecture. However, you'll want to make sure that the woodshed's positioning, materials, and ventilation are appropriate. The unit's front wall should face south and slope at close to a 45-degree angle. Use clear walls to let the sun in and black plastic or painted plywood inside to absorb heat. Side vents at the top pull warm air up past the wood, carrying moisture out the top.

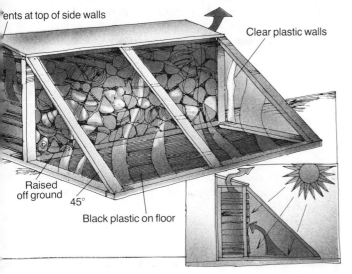

ents at top of side walls

Clear plastic walls

Raised off ground

45°

Black plastic on floor

Food...for Next Winter, Next Week

"Putting by" plenty in pantries, larders, root cellars

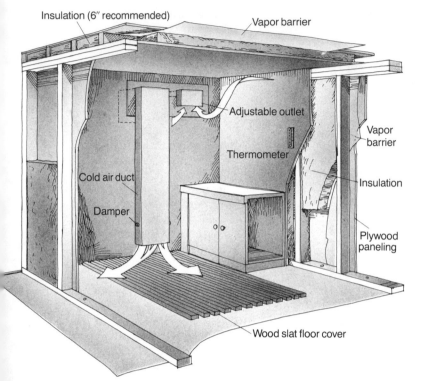

Insulation (6" recommended)

Vapor barrier

Adjustable outlet

Vapor barrier

Thermometer

Insulation

Cold air duct

Plywood paneling

Damper

Wood slat floor cover

Home cornucopia: a food cellar

To build a food cellar in your basement, partition off an area adjacent to a shaded north or east wall and away from heating ducts and pipes. Then insulate the ceiling, new interior walls, door, and (unless the climate is cool year-round) the exterior wall above ground level. Cool ground temperatures and, when the weather is cool, the outside air will keep cellar temperatures low; the insulation will keep out heated air from the living quarters. If possible, choose a site for your cellar with an outside opening—a window is convenient—to provide air flow. Install a cold air duct with a damper, and sliding outlet vent in the opening. A power fan and an automatic thermostat may be useful additions. A floor of sawdust sprinkled with water, with a platform of wood slats laid over it, will maintain humidity at the high level necessary for some food crops.

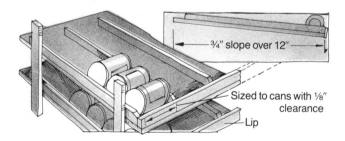

¾" slope over 12"

Sized to cans with ⅛" clearance

Lip

Cans roll right into reach

Food shelves that hold only bulk canned goods can be sloped forward so that cans will roll to the front. No more digging for buried cans—and the shelves can be as deep as you like. Molding strips laid across the front and along each shelf keep cans aligned.

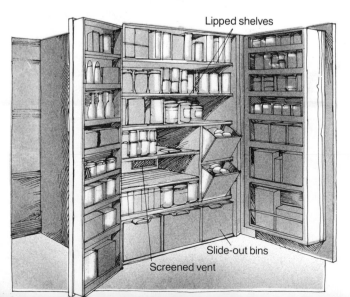

Lipped shelves

Slide-out bins

Screened vent

Granny's larder, revisited

If you'd like a multipurpose food storage area for canned goods, grains, cheeses, and bulk produce, revive an old tradition: the built-in larder. Lipped shelves hold canned goods, jars, and packaged foods securely; the double doors are lined with narrow shelves that provide additional—and highly accessible—storage. Down below, slide-out bins—a commercial system or homemade—hold fruits and vegetables. Screened vents to the outside or to a cool crawl space act as an old-time cooling device, keeping larder temperatures low.

Household food storage can be divided into two categories: pantry or room-temperature storage for canned goods and nonperishables; and root cellar cold storage for fruits, vegetables, staples, and preserves.

You can place cans and jars just about anywhere that's convenient (except near a furnace or water heater) in the garage or basement: on orderly shelves, inside an unused utility closet, or behind cabinet doors. However, most basements are too warm for root cellar storage. One way to bypass the temperature problem in a basement is to insulate a small area for food storage along a cool basement wall (see details shown at left and on page 78).

To cool the food storage area, you can use natural or mechanical methods (see page 77).

An old-fashioned root cellar with a cool dirt floor is another food storage option. Traditionally, root cellars were dug below the house, into the ground outside, or into a hillside. A modern-day crawl space may be just the place to locate your root cellar (see page 79 for ideas).

Most root crops require moist, cool storage conditions. Other crops, including winter squash and pumpkins, like warmer, drier surroundings. Consult an agricultural extension service for more detailed information about proper food storage. In addition, see the *Sunset* book *How to Grow Vegetables & Berries*.

Harvest headquarters

Metal utility shelves, durable and warp-resistant, are a practical choice for food storage. Lipped edges on the shelves hold jars safely. Adjustable—and available in many sizes—the shelves can be bolted to studs for added stability.

Contoured shelves offer simple-to-see storage

For maximum visibility, cans, jars, and bottles fit one or two-deep on narrow ends of contoured track-and-clip shelves above the counter. Bulkier items are stowed below. The counter is handy for unloading groceries—food goes right onto the shelves or into the freezer or extra refrigerator. The pantry floor is kept clear for the drop-down ladder.

Patio Paraphernalia

Bags of charcoal, comfortable cushions, sun umbrellas, hammocks, badminton and croquet sets, inner tubes and inflatable rafts — sometimes it seems we have as much furniture and equipment for the patio, deck, and pool as for the house. It's most convenient to store such things close to where you need them — wheeling the portable grill just a few feet makes spur-of-the-moment barbecues easier.

Most outdoor equipment does require shelter from an occasional summer shower. Closed storage units and roof or deck overhangs provide needed protection. Units should be built according to durable, waterproof designs, and from good materials: redwood, exterior plywood, and masonry are standards.

Patio, deck, and poolside storage should blend with or complement a house's architecture and landscaping.

Barbecues in dividers or against the house. The most durable barbecue is set into a freestanding unit built from brick, stone, or concrete blocks. Below the barbecue or to the side, you can build in cabinets for starter fluid, charcoal briquettes (in metal or plastic cans with tight-fitting lids to keep out moisture), utensils, and accessories. A barbecue-plus-storage unit often doubles as a divider wall, separating the patio area from the garden or yard.

Portable barbecues rust quickly when exposed to dampness and precipitation. A deep cabinet to house a portable barbecue can be built against the house wall, protected beneath the eaves. Barbecue storage cabinetry could include shelves, hanging pegs, and possibly drawers for tongs, mitts, and rotisseries; a fold-down door could double as a serving counter.

Using space beneath a deck. Even the space beneath a deck is often useful for storage. If yours is a low deck, consider a trap door with a built-in box below for hoses and gardening supplies. The trap door should match the decking materials; it can be set in place or attached with leaf-type hinges set flush with the deck. You might provide access to a larger below-deck space from the side; store lawn furniture or other large items there, protected from the weather.

Corner cabinets for outdoor activities

Barbecuing is a joy when the necessary cooking utensils are close at hand. The three double-door cabinets in this outdoor brick and tile barbecue center offer plenty of convenient storage space. The counter, a perfect buffet table for parties, doubles as a display surface for container plants. Design: Armstrong & Sharfman.

For storage, sunning, sitting

Hinged deck bench holds a cargo of gardening supplies. Solid to keep out the rain, the bench invites snoozing and sunbathing. Design: Ed Hoiland.

Disappearing act

Collapsible director's chairs tuck neatly and conveniently into an outside deck locker. The storage spot is actually space stolen from a corner cabinet in the kitchen. The well-camouflaged door was cut from the deck's wall paneling. Architects: Larsen, Lagerquist & Morris.

Furnishings, Offstage

Out of fashion or out of season, here's how to handle it

How can you make bulky belongings like dining room tables, overstuffed chairs, or china cabinets disappear? Unfortunately, there's no magical solution.

Most furniture is much too heavy or awkward to fit into standard storage units. You may be able to get lighter furnishings up onto overhead platforms (see page 65) or tuck them into "backwater" spots; but the best basic procedure for storing furniture is to keep it out of the traffic flow—in attic or basement corners and against walls—and arrange the pieces as compactly as possible.

Protect furniture by covering it with old mattress pads or blankets. Polyethylene sheeting, canvas, or even newspaper can also help keep the dust off. Lamps, decorations, and breakables should be stored on heavy-duty shelves.

See "Outdoor Furniture" (pages 32–33) and "Luggage & Game Tables" (pages 40–41) for more ideas.

Airy alley for all-purpose storage
Vinyl-coated-wire shelves are ideal for rugs and other storables that require good air circulation to prevent damage. Cartons fit on and under the shelves without blocking access to the back of the space. Architect: David Jeremiah Hurley.

Rugs require rolling

To store a rug or carpet for any length of time, roll it—never fold it—around a pole or cardboard tube. Wrap the carpet in paper or plastic, but leave some room for air to circulate. For rugs and carpets, the storage environment shouldn't be damp or overly warm: excessive drying is as bad as mildew. Moth balls or crystals will help keep insects away, but some fibers react adversely to these repellents. Consult a carpet expert before storing a prized carpet.

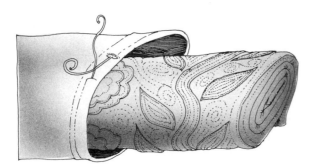

Quality quilt care

Ideally, heirloom quilts or fine blankets should be rolled or loosely folded, then inserted into a clean, all-cotton pillow-case or a larger covering made from a sheet. Never store a quilt in a plastic bag (the fibers need to breathe), and keep quilts from direct contact with wood. Take your quilts out of their cases occasionally and refold a different way.

Managing bed bulk

Keep your mattresses and box springs off the floor, and don't let them sag. Stand them upright against a wall. Prop them up with a large sheet of plywood or hardboard, or the bed's own headboard and slats; and secure the whole assembly against the wall, if necessary, with loops of wire, light chain, or rope attached to the wall behind.

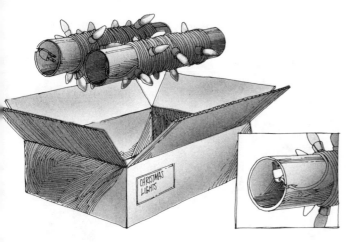

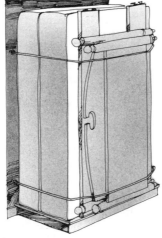

Tangle-free Christmas tip

Here's a way to save aggravation next year when you un-pack the Christmas tree lights. This year, save the cardboard tubes from rolls of gift wrapping paper and a few small-to-medium cardboard boxes. Cut the tubes to box length; then push each light strand's plug inside a tube end and secure with masking tape. Coil the lights firmly around the tube, as shown, by rotating the tube; tape the end in place. Tubes then slip snugly inside the box.

A 12-inch-long box and tube will handle a strand of 35 to 50 small twinkle lights. Use a larger box for a big-bulb strand.

Outdoor Furniture

Fair-weather forecast for longer-lasting beauty, service

When the weather prediction is "weekend showers," do you hope for sunny skies because you don't want to move your patio furniture? Whether the weather takes you by surprise or it's time to prepare for a change in season, you need convenient ways and protective places to store your outdoor furniture.

Hang lightweight objects on garage or basement walls, or place them on a loft platform or overhead rack, or inside carport storage units. If necessary, store bulky items in a garden shed (see pages 42–43), patio storage unit (see pages 28–29) or garage extension (see page 67).

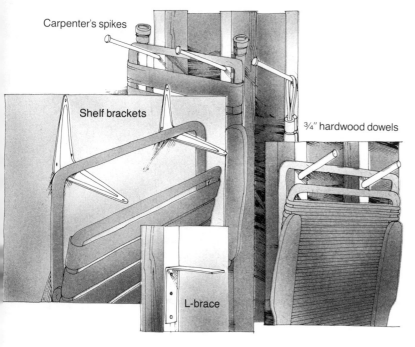

Carpenter's spikes

Shelf brackets

¾" hardwood dowels

L-brace

For fold-ups, easy hang-ups

Save precious floor space by hanging lightweight folding lawn chairs and recliners from wall studs, on ceiling joists, or even high on the rafters. For simple supports, use carpenter's spikes (oversized nails) driven into framing members, or ¾-inch dowels glued and inserted into predrilled holes; common shelf brackets or L-braces are other possibilities. Arrange supports in pairs that fit each piece.

A simple track-and-bracket system, intended for shelving, can also be used for storing furniture on the walls.

High-rise storage for window sections

Storm sashes, screens, and window shades are safely out of the way when placed on parallel wood racks suspended from ceiling joists or rafters. Racks for heavy storm windows should be assembled with bolts; racks for lightweight screens can be built with nails or screws. The hardware on sashes prohibits flat stacking; offset every other sash an inch or two. A similar rack is shown in the photo at the bottom of page 13.

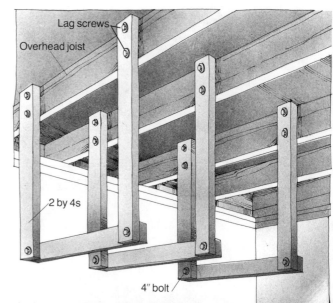

Lag screws

Overhead joist

2 by 4s

4" bolt

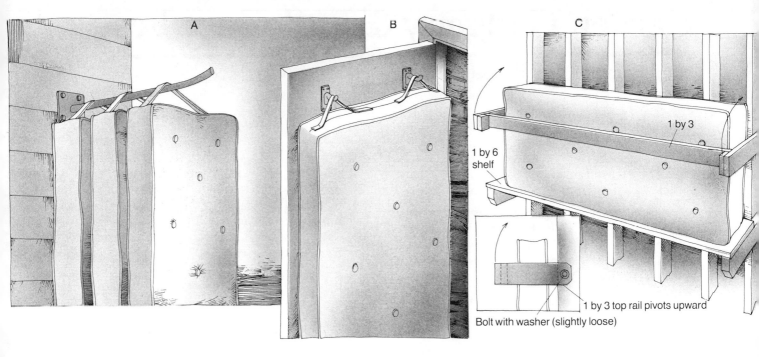

1 by 3

1 by 6 shelf

1 by 3 top rail pivots upward

Bolt with washer (slightly loose)

Airy care for outdoor cushions

Those colorful and comfy cushions deserve some attention when it comes to storage. With a heavy summer storm or the first fall freeze, it's time to bring outdoor furniture cushions inside.

Cushions should be stored off the ground to provide good air circulation, promote quick drying, and prevent mildew problems. A wrought iron rod (A) attached to a wall stud is a handy device for hanging several cushions from their hand loops or from loops you've sewn in place. Metal coat hooks (B) hold individual cushions. Build horizontal racks from fir or pine (C) for long chaise lounge pads; attach the racks to open studs. The upper rail pivots.

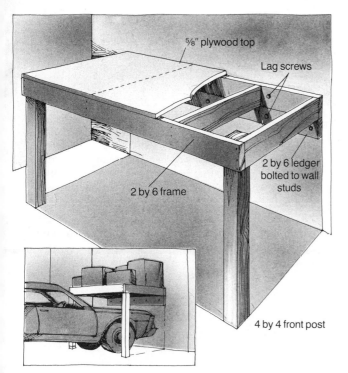

5/8" plywood top

Lag screws

2 by 6 frame

2 by 6 ledger bolted to wall studs

4 by 4 front post

Up and away in a loft

Get on top of the storage situation by placing patio tables and pool furniture under the garage roof—or better yet, over the car. If you and a helper can lift the furniture, store it on this loft platform. The back of the platform sits on a ledger strip, which is attached to wall studs or to a masonry wall. The front of the platform is supported by sturdy posts that straddle the car hood. For more information and ideas about loft storage, see page 65.

Garden Gadgetry & Bulk Supplies

Pruning shears to potting soil ... a place for everything

Whether you keep small garden tools in the garage or garden shed, you need handy and safe storage.

A pegboard and hanger system is ideal for organizing light to medium-weight tools and supplies. Closed cabinets are best for garden poisons, sprayers, and extra-sharp tools—keep your cabinets locked if small children are afoot.

If you're putting your garden center to bed for the winter, tools need an environment where they won't rust. If rust-producing dampness is a problem, treat tools with liquid rust cleaner, emery paper, or a wire brush; then oil any working parts and apply a light coating of grease to surfaces likely to rust again. Fertilizers, potting soils, and chemicals should be sealed from moisture inside bins or cabinets; metal containers help keep rodents and insects out of grass seed and bird feed.

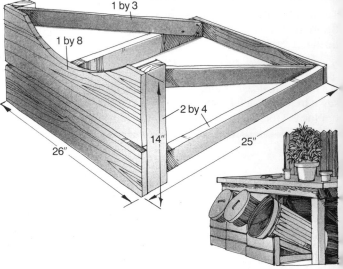

Keeping hoses unsnarled

Wrestling with the garden hose can often be a muddy, tangled proposition. One solution is a reel, mounted next to a water outlet inside a garden shed, garage, or basement. A 20-inch length of 2-inch PVC pipe runs through the wall leading to the garden; you just reel in the hose when it's not in use.

To organize hose nozzles and accessories, drill recesses with a 1¼-inch Foerstner bit into a length of 2 by 4; you could fit the board between wall studs near the hose, or mount it to a wall or fence with L-braces.

Storing soil additives

Tucked beneath a potting table or workbench, these containers make a handy, space-saving addition to any gardening center. Use them to store peat moss, potting soil, sand, and fertilizers. Lay garbage cans atop a slanting wooden rack, as shown; from there, your materials can be transferred directly to pot or wheelbarrow. This rack could be built with a third board across the front to increase the angle.

Sunlit shelving for potted plants

Plywood shelving under the large greenhouse window provides storage space for empty pots and saucers below, and a convenient counter on top. Attached to wall studs, the sturdy potting shelf at left is at comfortable working height; there's room below for large bags of lawn fertilizer. The high shelves hold miscellaneous supplies. The window in this garden storage area bathes plants with light; the plastic roof and swinging plastic panel overhead keep the corner warm. Architects: Sortun • Vos Partnership.

Heavy Garden Gear

Big and ungainly machines and tools need space, easy access

Large and bulky garden equipment—power mowers, mini-tractors, rototillers, sprayers, and snowblowers —usually requires a spacious, sheltered floor area (dry to prevent rust) and a clear path to the access door. On the subject of doors: they must be wide enough for your biggest piece of machinery, and the sills must be low, or you'll have to build a ramp or two.

If your equipment inventory is growing steadily, consider building a garden shed (see pages 42–43) or a garage extension (see page 67).

Easy wheeling into the back yard

Gardening equipment rolls conveniently onto a brick walkway through a large sliding door at the back of the garage. Architect: Thomas Jon Rosengren, Inc.

Dowels prop long-handled tools

Brooms, shovels, cultivators, and other garden tools stay vertical, thanks to dowel dividers in this roomy carport closet, just a short walk away from flower and vegetable gardens. The remaining floor space accommodates a garden sprayer and sacks of charcoal. When closed, the sliding doors blend with the wall of the carport. Architect: Buzz Bryan.

Wall space, floor space, even shelf space

Nails in wooden walls do the work of brackets, holding garden equipment. A single shelf stores garden supplies that otherwise might clutter up valuable floor space, reserved here for a mower and bags of potting soil and manure. Architects: Moyer Associates Architects.

Laundry Needs

Tips to save you time, fuss, and mismatched socks

Storage units and accessories above and around your washer and dryer make an efficient work area. Place a long, deep shelf—or shelves—directly above the machines for frequently used supplies. Above the shelf is a perfect spot to install ceiling-high cabinets for cleaning supplies, linens, and overflow storage.

Every laundry area needs counter space for folding, sorting, sprinkling, and mending clothes. Plastic laminate counters are easy to clean. In cramped quarters, a fold-down counter is convenient. You may also want a sink for washing delicate garments or soaking out stains. Hang clothes for drip-drying on a simple metal or wooden closet rod over the sink. A ceiling fan directly above promotes quick drying.

Install more cabinets or a set of large-capacity storage bins below the counter. On the wall attach a narrow cabinet for your ironing board. Close off the area with louvered double doors: they hide clutter and muffle the noise of machines while providing adequate ventilation.

Laundry layover

Custom-fitted to an odd-shaped area in the basement laundry room, these wide-open shelves are a vital link in the laundry assembly line. The cubicles, made of particle board and faced with fir, hold washing supplies and folded laundry; blouses go right on hangers. Architects: Sortun • Vos Partnership.

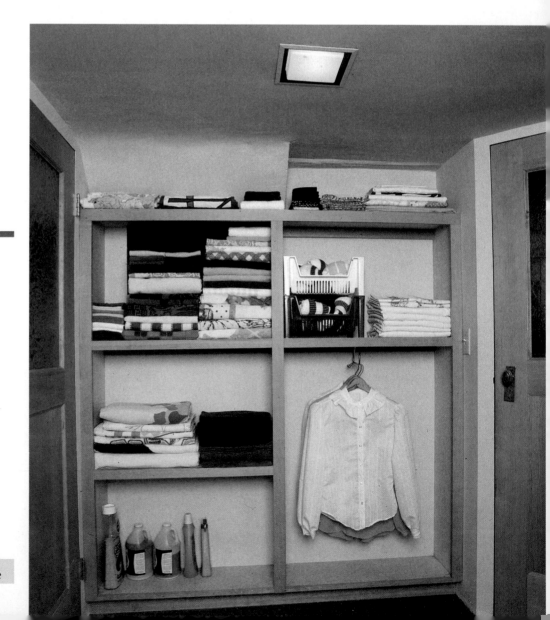

Out-of-sight ironing board

A full-size ironing board can be stored inside a storage closet near the laundry or in a shallow cabinet of its own. In a storage closet, secure the board with a chain or strap. For greater convenience, build a special slot for the board. A cabinet built to house an ironing board alone should allow several inches around the board for access. The average board would fit in a space 65 inches tall, 21 inches wide, and 5 inches deep; but dimensions vary, so be sure to measure your board.

Built-in ironing boards commonly fold down from behind a door, or pivot or slide out from a slot below the counter top.

Add an electrical outlet inside your board compartment or nearby for your iron.

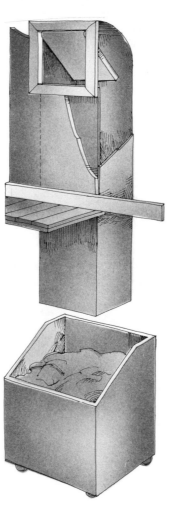

More fun than bother ...a laundry chute

A laundry chute effortlessly directs dirty clothes from your home's main or second floor to a laundry center in the basement or garage below. You can locate the chute opening in an inconspicuous but handy spot—inside a clothes closet in the master bedroom; in a wall, with a hinged or flap door; or inside a bathroom cabinet. If you have curious youngsters on the loose, be sure that the opening is raised high above the floor or measures no more than 12 inches across.

The best time to think "laundry chute," of course, is when you're designing or remodeling your house. Materials? Plywood, sheet aluminum, or 18-inch-diameter furnace heating duct (look in the Yellow pages under "Furnaces," "Sheet Metal Work," or "Plumbing Contractors").

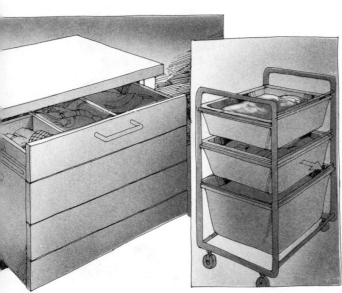

Order out of clothing chaos

Whether below a counter, inside a freestanding island, or stacked floor to ceiling, sorting bins keep clothes ready to go when laundry day arrives. Have at least three large bins for sorting whites, colors, and permanent press items; a fourth bin might hold towels or work clothes.

Below the counter, try wooden tilt-out bins or one large pull-out drawer with internal compartments. Against the wall, you could use a commercial system with bins that slide out of their own frames, or improvise with plastic dish bins on wooden drawer guides (see page 55). A roll-around hamper, or removable bins, can go right with you wherever they're needed.

Luggage & Game Tables

Often awkward to fit anywhere—but here are solutions

Whether you spend your free time traveling to faraway places or enjoying ping-pong or poker at home, you'll face pretty much the same storage problem: because of their special sizes and shapes, neither luggage nor game tables fit neatly into regular cabinets and closets. All too often, these items are stacked clumsily against a wall or take up space in the wrong place.

To store card or ping-pong tables, train or game boards, and suitcases during the off season, you might look for out-of-the-way ledges; or build enclosures specially tailored to their dimensions; or construct a high-up platform. With a pulley system, you can even pull an unwieldy table or trunk up out of the way without having to build a platform.

Tailor-built hideaways

Card tables and folding chairs—for morning bridge parties, late-night poker games, and Sunday afternoon barbecues —always pose a storage problem. It's wise to find them a spot of their own. Some convenient places are (A) inside a cubbyhole cabinet below a staircase; (B) in a narrow, deep slot at the back of a garage storage wall; and (C) in a tilt-out bin built into a cabinet. These places work well for luggage, too.

Before building a cabinet or otherwise modifying a storage area, measure your tables, chairs and luggage. Collapsible tables and chairs require very little depth; luggage needs a little more. Most square tables come in sizes up to 36 inches square, and round tables are usually 30 to 36 inches in diameter. A folded chair is usually 20 to 22 inches wide and up to 38 inches high. Make your hideaway snug enough for tables to stand upright, but allow several spare inches of clearance in width and height for access.

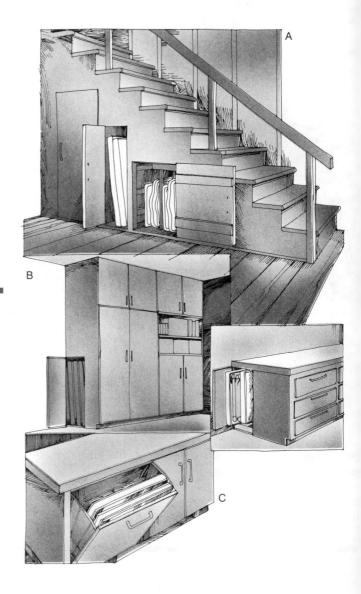

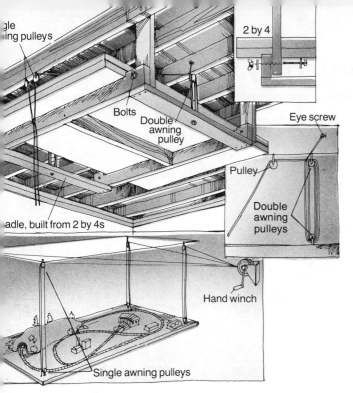

ngle
ring pulleys

Bolts
Double
awning
pulley

2 by 4

Eye screw

Pulley

Double
awning
pulleys

adle, built from 2 by 4s

Hand winch

Single awning pulleys

Winch-and-pulley hoist-ups

Nothing eats up basement or garage space like a ping-pong table or model train board. A hand pulley system, or a hand winch and pulleys, can give such storables a big lift. At top, a folded ping-pong table is set onto a wood cradle, then hoisted to the ceiling and secured there with bolts. The train board shown below has matching single awning pulleys above and below, and is raised with a small hand winch. It's always best to have two people around when it's time to hoist your table or board.

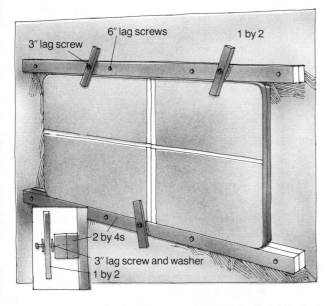

3" lag screw

6" lag screws

1 by 2

2 by 4s

3" lag screw and washer

1 by 2

Put a wall to work

If you have spare wall space inside or a roof-protected space outdoors on the leeward side of the house, here's a basic rack that will hold your ping-pong or card table securely. Nail parallel rails of doubled 2 by 4s across wall studs. Make the space between the rails equal to your table's width plus ¼ inch for clearance. Eight-inch lengths of fir 1 by 2 pivot on lag screws and washers to hold the table in place. To store tables more than 3 inches thick, consider adapting the rack shown in drawing C on page 33.

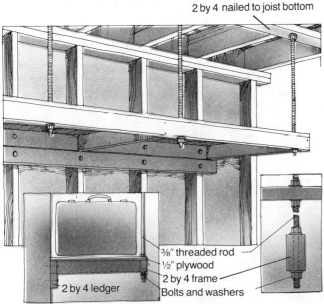

2 by 4 nailed to joist bottom

⅜" threaded rod
½" plywood
2 by 4 frame
2 by 4 ledger
Bolts and washers

Luggage line-up

Luggage and other bulky storage odds and ends line up along this secure ledge, which takes advantage of high wall space in garages or basements. The 38-inch-wide shelf sits atop a 2 by 4 ledger strip fastened to wall studs. It's supported in front by threaded rods tied into a 2 by 4 nailed across ceiling joists or rafters. Line the ledge with carpet scraps to avoid scraping luggage.

Sheds for Storage Overflow

A separate shed serves two storage purposes: garden and yard gear can be near to where you use them, and more space is available in the garage, attic, and basement.

Simple or elaborate, a shed can be a model of efficiency and convenience, actually making it easy to transplant petunias or put away the tricycle.

Check local building codes

Before setting your sights on a certain kind of shed, visit the building inspector in your area. You'll need to find out whether to apply for a building permit and what codes affect your project. Detached buildings are often subject to requirements regarding minimum setbacks from property lines. You may also face limits on installing water and electrical lines or be required to build your shed with fire-retardant materials. Codes vary: sheds aren't allowed in some communities; in others, you can locate a shed almost anywhere on your property, as long as it isn't anchored to the ground or set on a concrete slab.

Should you buy or build?

Depending on how industrious you are, you can erect a metal shed frame from a kit, assemble the parts of a prefab unit, or build your shed from scratch.

If you choose the metal frame, you'll play the roles of a mechanic and carpenter. You can also select what kind of siding and roofing to use: wood, aluminum, fiberglass, or heavy translucent plastic. The heavy plastic can be used to create a greenhouse effect.

Convenient to install, prefab metal sheds come in standard designs; some can be assembled in an afternoon. However, they tend to rust, and it's difficult to attach storage units and accessories to their thin walls. So before buying a prefab kit, find out whether the manufacturer provides a line of shelves, racks, and other accessories especially designed for the metal shed. If accessories aren't available for the design you want, you can always build a wood frame inside the shed.

Wood frame sheds allow you to create an attractive custom design that meets your exact needs and suits your available space. You can easily attach storage units to wall studs or overhead rafters. Unlike a metal shed, a wood shed is flammable; and you'll have to devote considerable time to planning and building.

Shed specifications

A shed should be at least 6 feet wide and a minimum of 4 to 6 feet deep, depending on your needs. If you're building it, plan your access wisely. Install a wide door —4 to 5 feet.

If allowed by code, a shed should be on some kind of foundation to secure it from wind and frost heave. The foundation also prevents wood floors from rotting. Metal sheds often come without floors; a concrete slab is an ideal foundation for these. Some prefab sheds come with special ground anchors or floor supports. Concrete piers and wood beams make a simple, efficient foundation for a wood frame shed.

If your shed floor is above ground level or if the door has a high sill, you'll probably want to use some kind of ramp. A ramp makes access more convenient for wheeling in a wheelbarrow or driving in a mini-tractor. If the floor of the shed is on the ground, elevate equipment on concrete blocks in the winter.

Planning your shed's interior

The rule for storage in tight spaces like sheds is to keep small objects off the floor. Floor space is valuable, and you'll want to use it for access and heavy equipment. You can fasten cabinets, shelves, tool racks, and workbenches to the framing members in a wood shed. If you don't use the manufacturer's storage accessories for a metal shed, consider building a wood frame inside it.

To help you plan your shed's innards, review the following storage ideas:
• Old kitchen cabinets or a counter with built-in drawers are great for a mid-size shed.
• Garden poisons should be locked in a cabinet out of children's reach.
• If you have a hinged door that swings out, install narrow shelves on the back of the door.
• Industrial metal shelves can be used in a shed; they won't warp from dampness, but they may rust.

If your lawn chairs and other outdoor items won't take up all of your shed space, incorporate a garden work center into the shed. Set up a potting counter, and provide garbage cans or tilt-out bins for fertilizer and potting materials; a sink; racks for tools and pots; and small shelves for seeds and bottles. Hang a chalkboard on the wall to record planting timetables and schedule weekly garden duties. See pages 34–37 for specific ideas on storing garden tools and supplies.

Tree-side potting nest

Set against a backdrop of towering redwoods, this potting shed repeats the design and materials of the adjacent struc- tures. The doorway, partial walls, and slatted roof contribute to the open feeling and let light into the shed, making it ideal for growing plants from seeds. Potting supplies fit on shelves that run the length of one shed wall. Along the other walls are a work counter, a utility sink, and below-counter bins.

Summer Sports Gear

Ready when you are: boats, bats, balls, rackets, fins, tackle

Summer sports equipment ranges in size from the compact softball to the 16-foot canoe. You'll have to vary your storage methods accordingly. You may want to rotate summer sports equipment by season: keep baseballs and swim fins in less accessible spots during winter months and within easy reach during the height of summer activities.

Some sporting goods, such as baseball bats, tennis rackets, and water-skis, can be stored on organized racks or pegboards. Equestrians might hang bridles and bits on hooks and pegs, and saddles on horizontal "saddleback" rails made with 2 by 4s. For organizing a variety of items of various sizes and shapes—such as

camping and fishing gear—shelves, closets, and storage chests are the most convenient. A stack of deep cubbyhole shelves by the garage door keeps gear immediately accessible. For the dedicated athlete, metal school lockers—either new or recycled—make familiar storage units. A simple nylon hammock strung overhead can keep basketballs, footballs, and sleeping bags from disappearing.

Very light boats can be hung on ropes or racks attached to inside or outside walls; canoes and rowboats are often suspended from overhead joists or collar beams—providing they can handle the weight. For storing heavy or large boats, see pages 50–51.

Angled walls for rifles and poles

Racks mounted on angular corner walls offer out-of-the-way places to store rifles and fishing poles, keeping these items accessible, yet removed from the rest of the garage. Because only fishing nets and boots are on the floor, the storeroom door can swing open without banging into any equipment.

Chains and frame cradle canoe

Attached to the rafters with chains, a strong wood frame supports this heavy canoe and keeps it out of the way of cars. Neatly stacked firewood functions as a windbreak at the back of the carport. Architect: James Van Drimmelen.

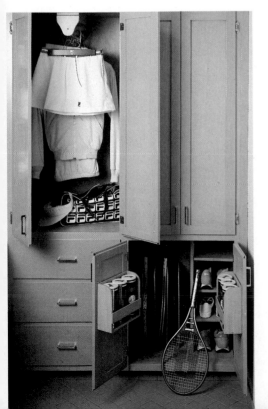

An ace of a storage place

Custom cabinetry keeps tennis equipment and running gear neatly packed away. Sets of double doors open into mini-clothes lockers with room for bags at the bottom. The lower unit is fitted with cubbies for shoes, dividers for rackets, and racks for cans of tennis balls. Design: Betsie Corwin and William G. Florence.

Winter Sports Equipment

Safe stashing of skis, skates, saucers, sleds

During the winter, you might want to keep your seasonal sports gear where it's ready for a quick weekend trip to the mountains or a morning visit to the slopes. In the spring, winter equipment can trade places with golf clubs, baseball bats, or camping equipment, and go into less accessible areas—up into attic corners, against the ridge line or rafters, or into a crawl space.

The rule for most winter storables, in and out of season, is to hang them up. Skis are easily hung by the pair or grouped in a rack. Snowshoes, saucers, skates, and small sleds are best hung on nails, spikes, pegs, or hooks (see page 7). Toboggans and bigger sleds can rest atop raised platforms, ceiling joists, or collar beams.

Short steps from ski locker to car

Packing up for skiing is simple when the ski equipment is behind double doors in the carport. Skis, poles, and a ski rack rest on dowels in this long, shallow closet. Boots go on the floor. Architects: The Hastings Group.

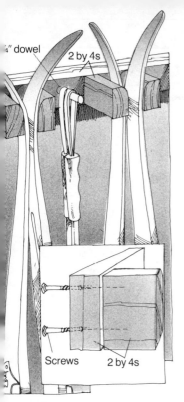

Block-and-peg ski rack

Because skis conveniently curve at the tips, they'll hang from many kinds of blocks or runners spaced 1¼ inches or so apart. This simple and effective ski rack uses short blocks cut from a 2 by 4 of oak, pine, fir, or redwood. The blocks are glued and screwed to a longer 2 by 4 backing piece. Ski poles hang on adjacent recessed dowels. To add a finishing touch, and to protect skis from scratches, round off and sand smooth the inside top corner of each block. Finish the rack with penetrating resin or polyurethane varnish.

Overhead joist

Making the most of joists and beams

Open ceiling joists or collar beams supply a ready-to-use storage spot for sleds, saucers, and other outdoor equipment: simply rest the runners across a couple of joists. Another idea is to hang snowshoes and skates from nails, spikes, pegs, or hooks sunk into the joists.

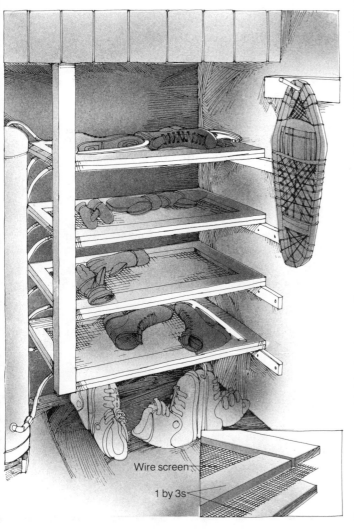

Wire screen

1 by 3s

Drying out that soggy gear

When you get home from the slopes or the pond, you head for the warmth of the fire...but where do you put your cold, damp ski boots, skates, snowshoes, gloves, and socks?

These drying and storage shelves, adjacent to the water heater for extra drying power, are built from wire screen sandwiched by two 1 by 3 frames; the screens allow air to circulate and moisture to drip. For even quicker drying, run copper tubing—heated by the water heater— underneath each shelf.

Guard Against Storage Hazards

Open boxes spilling over with useless papers, a rickety ladder propped in a corner, carelessly placed sharp tools — these hazards deserve attention. If you're setting your storage in order, make room for safety, too.

Garages, attics, and basements are very susceptible to accident and fire. To prevent storage disasters, your first jobs are to sort, organize, and clean. Discard old paint cans, broken toys, and other unneeded items.

Following are some specific pointers and suggestions to help you with your task. For more safety guidelines, contact fire, health, and other appropriate officials.

Organize your workshop

A clean workshop is a safe workshop. Make it a habit to frequently discard wood scraps and vacuum up sawdust, especially behind panels, boxes, and equipment where highly flammable sawdust collects.

Power tools present a host of dangers. Power tools and lighting should be on separate circuits; a tool circuit should be at least 20 amps to prevent overload. Grounded (three-prong) outlets are a necessity. Also, don't use power tools in damp conditions. A master switch controlled by a key is a wise precaution. To guard against shock, purchase double-insulated power tools.

Make sure that your workshop has sufficient lighting (see page 66) and that the floor is clear of items that could cause a fall.

Guard garden supplies

Your garage or garden shed makes a perfect secret place for little ones playing hide-and-seek. Children—yours or your neighbor's — can easily get into toxic garden supplies or play with sharp tools if these items aren't properly stored.

Place dangerous tools and poisons well out of children's reach. Hang sharp tools high on walls with strong hooks; make sure they won't fall. Tools can also be stored, along with toxic substances, in drawers and cabinets that have plastic "childproof" latches (see drawing below left) or metal locks. Do not store poisons under utility sinks, on the ground between wall studs, or near bulk food supplies. Remember, pets should be protected from these dangers, too.

Ladders and staircases: watch your step

Ladders and staircases should be adequate for the loads you'll be carrying up and down them, and should always be in good condition. Never block a ladder or staircase with boxes or overflow storage.

Position a ladder so that its base is offset from the perpendicular by ¼ of its length (the foot of a 20-foot ladder, for example, should be 5 feet from the point directly beneath the top of the ladder). Fold-down ladders usually aren't intended for heavy use; buy one with minimum bounce.

Handrails on staircases should be solidly secured, and the steps clear and well lighted, with light switches at the top and bottom. A minimum of 6½ feet of headroom all the way up is often required by code.

Be cautious with heating equipment

Make sure that combustibles are not positioned near heating equipment such as a furnace, water heater, heating ducts, or a chimney.

Store ashes in a metal container; don't place ashes in cardboard boxes or in a place where a breeze can stir up embers.

It's wise to have a professional inspect and clean your heating equipment every year. Do not leave portable heaters unattended, or place them where they can be tipped over.

Avoid electrical problems

Plugging too many tools or appliances into an extension cord is hazardous because the cord's insulation can ignite. Generally, do not rely heavily on extension cords. You can start a fire by stringing extension cords

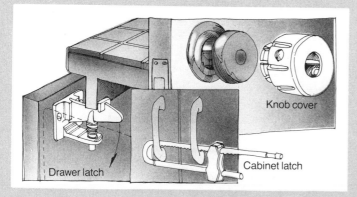

Knob cover

Drawer latch

Cabinet latch

under rugs, tying them to nails, or using extra-long cords of insufficient gauge. Periodically inspect extension cords for cracks, fraying, and broken plugs.

Check with an electrician to make sure that your circuits aren't overloaded; you may need to install additional circuits in your basement or garage workshop, or in your attic for lighting.

Isolate flammable liquids

Storing flammable liquids is a risky practice. Gasoline for lawnmowers and other equipment should be stored in a safety can (see drawing below) with a spring closure valve, vapor vent, pouring spout, and the label of a testing laboratory. Paint, solvent, rubber cement, and other flammable substances should be stored in metal cans with tight-fitting lids in a well-ventilated area far away from heat sources. Never store flammable liquids in glass, plastic, or makeshift containers.

It's a good idea to place correctly containered liquids in a metal cabinet. Do not store them in the house; the vapors that escape from cans are often dangerous. Rags that have soaked up flammable substances should also be kept in metal containers with tight-fitting lids away from heat sources. Better yet, throw them away.

Be sure to clean up any oil drippings.

Pouring spout

Testing lab label

Spring closure valve

Vapor vent

Install lifesaving devices

Smoke and heat detectors, automatic sprinklers, fire extinguishers, and modifications of attic fans can make your storage areas much safer. Other safety measures include solid-core doors (which slow the spread of fire) leading from a carport or garage into living space, and fire-retardant material covering insulation.

Smoke and heat detectors set off an alarm to alert people to danger, giving them time to escape. Smoke detectors alone, when properly placed, installed, and maintained, offer the minimum level of safety recommended by the National Fire Protection Association. Used in conjunction with a smoke detector, a home heat detector is particularly useful in an attached garage, attic, or basement. Heat detectors react when the air reaches a certain temperature, usually 135° F.

An automatic sprinkler system, typically seen in public buildings, is used with a smoke detector or other automatic alarm. A small sprinkler system provides protection in the vulnerable areas of your home: the garage, attic, and basement.

Sprinklers are designed to slow the development and spread of fire. A drawback of a sprinkler system, of course, is that water might damage valuables.

Fire extinguishers. Fire emergencies require quick action. Keep a multipurpose chemical fire extinguisher (see drawing) in or near your garage, attic, or basement. Make sure that the extinguisher carries the UL label of approval and is inspected yearly.

The only times you should try to put out a fire by yourself are when you're near the fire when it begins, or when you discover the fire in its early stages. And, of course, you must know how to use an extinguisher. Don't be overly ambitious in the face of fire; your personal safety comes first.

An attic fan can be a lethal instrument if a fire starts anywhere in your house while the fan is in operation. Air currents speed combustion, and can turn a small fire into a raging one in a few seconds. To eliminate this hazard, fit the louvered shutters on fans with fusible links, and equip fan power circuits with an automatic cut-off switch activated by a fire detection system.

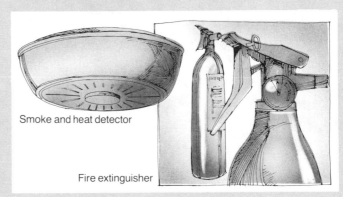

Smoke and heat detector

Fire extinguisher

Trailers, RVs & Boats

Great fun on the go, a sizeable challenge back home

Recreational vehicles, camper trailers, and boats on trailers are difficult to hide. To make matters more complex, many local ordinances demand that all trailers and RVs be off the street and out of sight. Your storage options include the back or side yard behind a fence, the garage (if possible), an independent structure, or an extension of the house or garage. (Before building a structure, check with local building officials.)

The big problem with most RVs is their height. The average garage door opening is 7 feet high; RVs demand clearance of up to 10 feet. Your boat trailer or camper trailer may fit inside a standard garage if you're willing to steal space from the family car.

Smaller boats without trailers can hang on a wall or overhead (see page 45). Larger boats share the same drawbacks as RVs and trailers.

Outboard motors for boats should be stored upright and off the floor, in a dry, ventilated garage, basement, or shed. Collar beams or ceiling joists are excellent for storing masts and booms.

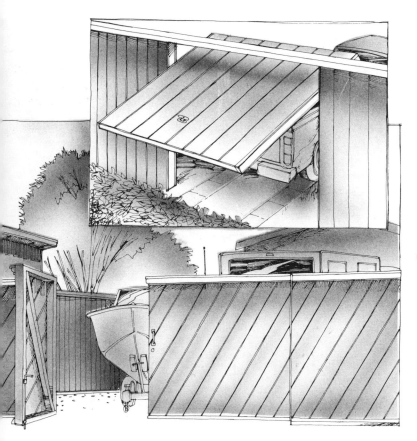

Invisible gates for sleek street view

To conceal a boat or camper trailer in a wide side yard, construct a special access gate that blends with the surroundings and presents only a smooth, continuous fence line when viewed from the street.

For your gate or set of gates, use overhead door hardware with a heavy-duty gate frame if your trailer isn't too high, lightweight gates that lift out of place, or standard hinged gates. The gate siding should match the adjoining fence exactly.

Don't ruin your camouflage with a paved driveway at the access area. Most lawns can handle occasional traffic; plant a sturdy ground cover, if necessary. For extra lawn protection when you need to move your trailer, lay down runners made from old plywood sheets.

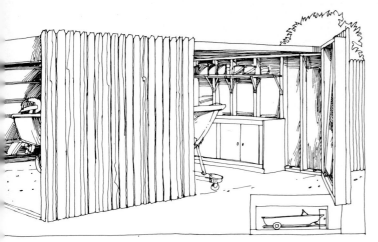

Custom garage—costly but most protective

Though expensive, a new structure is the most protective way to house your RV, camper trailer, or boat. Shown here is an unobtrusive, flat-topped garage built against a back fence—the siding and doors match the fence materials, and the structure doesn't rise above the neighborhood fence line. Inside there's electrical power, as well as a workbench and room for water-skis and boat accessories.

Another option for a boat or trailer is a garage or house extension (see page 67) with large double doors for access, and storage space behind and above.

Waterside garages: a gift of height

The divided garage complex in this home has something most garages don't—height. That's what the owner had in mind when designing it. The added height in the garages provides the necessary space for parking a trailer, RV, or boat.

Workshop Basics

Consider safety first, then organize for project efficiency

The four major components of an efficient home workshop are the workbench, storage units, proper lighting, and adequate electrical wiring and outlets. (For a discussion of lighting and wiring considerations, see pages 48–49 and 66.)

The focus of your workshop should be a large, stable workbench. Many kinds are available premade, or you can make your own from a 2 by 4 frame and plywood or hardboard top. The area beneath a workbench is ideal for drawers, cabinets, boxes, and shelves.

Storage units and stationary power tools should be ordered in a way that reflects the sequence of a typical project. Similar tools and materials should be grouped together so that you can find them easily. Large power tools mounted on casters can be rolled out from a stor-

age closet or cabinet, or away from a wall, then back again when the work is done. Wall cabinets are best for portable power tools because they protect the blades and working parts from damage and keep children from making dangerous mischief.

Besides tools and projects in progress, you'll want to store materials: leftover lumber, metal scraps, or bulk lumber from a special sale. Leftovers can be stored in a rolling box with a hinged top. Shelf brackets fastened to every other wall stud will handle light lumber. For heavier loads, assemble "ladder racks," like the ones used at lumberyards, from 2 by 4s and lag screws. Tough fiber storage tubes help pigeonhole and protect lengths of pipe or moldings. And if you're pressed for space, look to the rafters or ceiling joists.

Plywood shelves hold plenty

Good planning takes the spotlight in this woodworker's den. Graduated shelves on sturdy brackets keep lengthy timbers out of the way. When it's time to cut them down to size with the table saw, an outside door is opened to make room for any wood overhang. Lights fitted on overhead tracks illuminate the workbench and table saw; heat lamps help dry lamination projects. Architect: J. Alexander Riley.

Pristine platform workshop

Elevated on a 4½-inch-high concrete slab at the rear of the
garage, this workshop makes efficient use of walls and floor
space. Hand tools on the pegboard panels are conveniently
within reach. Mounted on the left wall is a cabinet with small
drawers for organizing nails, screws, hooks, and other
supplies. A wall-mounted strip with outlets every 15 inches
provides electricity for power tools on casters. The outlets are
controlled by a key-operated switch, keeping youngsters
from playing with the equipment. Architect: R. Gary Allan.

Workshop Hand Tools & Supplies

Maintaining order for a miscellany of small items

Hammers, paint cans, motor oil, nails, picture hooks, electrical fuses, extension cords: home maintenance supplies get out of hand fast without neat organization. And a home workshop can also mean woodworking, crafts, art, or darkroom supplies to store. What you need are storage containers and units that corral easily lost small items in specific, accessible places. The ideal workshop should combine both open and closed storage.

Hand tools are among the most bothersome workshop storables. The popular pegboard and hanger system (see pages 7 and 53) is best suited for visible, hands-on storage. You can also buy individual wall racks for small tools like screwdrivers and pliers.

Though less accessible, closed units protect tools from rust and dust. One space-saving closed unit is a shallow cabinet with sturdy double doors: line the cabinet back and both doors with tools.

Less-often-used storables, such as paint, brake fluid, and turpentine, can go on shelves installed high on the wall or suspended overhead or between ceiling joists. Graduate your shelf depth and spacing to fit the containers—gallons, quarts, and pints—and make sure that the labels are visible.

Drawers—plenty of them—are a blessing to any workshop owner. Build them into your work counters or an open frame, or recycle old bedroom dressers or kitchen units.

Dream home for fasteners

Fasteners of every size, type, and description can easily be spotted inside carefully labeled bins. Hinged doors in the top cabinet unit flip up for access, down for protection and neat appearance. The base cabinet is headquarters for painting supplies, and on the countertop are parts drawers—for even more fasteners.

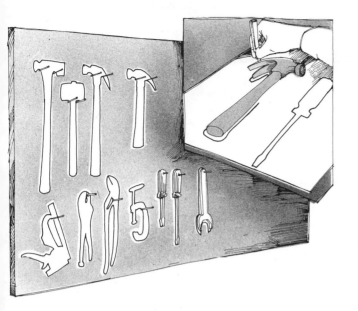

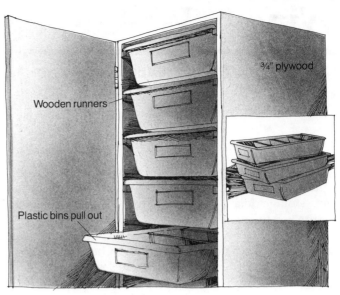

Instant guide to what goes where

It's no small task to keep hand tools in order and accounted for, especially when several family members share the same workshop. These simple silhouettes will help.

The simplest way to make silhouettes is to hang your tools in the ideal order, then outline each one with a broad-tipped indelible felt pen. Or lay each tool on heavy white paper and trace its outline. Carefully cut out each silhouette and glue it to the wall as shown. The glued-on silhouettes will last longer if you coat the entire board with clear sealer.

Slide-out supply bins

These sturdy plastic bins—purchased from office, restaurant, or school suppliers—are just right for home maintenance or crafts supplies. Build a plywood frame, then attach pairs of small wooden runners to both side walls as shown. Bins slide or lift out for easy access. For extra protection or just to be fancy, add a hinged door to the entire unit.

Cutlery trays, though less rugged, also make serviceable drawers or fine workshop drawer inserts.

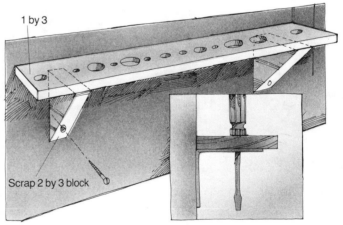

Natty solutions for nuts, bolts, nails

Jars, empty coffee cans, and cigar boxes can help save your workshop from chaos. House these containers on narrow shelves lipped with 1 by 2 trim. Jars for nails, nuts, and other items unscrew from their own lids, which are fastened to the bottoms of the lipped shelves.

Between-stud shelves with 1 by 4 or 1 by 6 strips across the fronts are also ideal for small storage.

Quick-reach tool rack

One simple way to keep small hand tools such as screwdrivers, files, or chisels instantly accessible is to build a tool rack at the rear of your workbench. Drill holes through a length of 1 by 3, large enough for each tool's shank to pass through, but too small for the handle. Attach your rack to the wall with L-braces or triangular blocks made from scraps of 2 by 4.

Wine in Waiting

Laying aside a few valued bottles—or aging by the case

If you're serious about your wines, you'll soon want an organized, stable environment (see pages 58–59 for wine storage details) for your collection. Racks or bins are the key to organizing your wines.

Will you store a few bottles for ready consumption or a by-the-case collection that requires bottle aging? For relatively few bottles, commercial accordion or cubbyhole racks are commonly available at department stores and at some wine shops. Diamond-shaped or triangular bins are traditional for long-term storage (see photo, page 59); the typical bin has a capacity of one to one and a half cases. Wine bottles of any size up to a magnum (2 quarts) may be stored on cabinet shelves or open shelves 14 inches deep.

When it comes to designing your own racks, remember two things: racks must be sturdy (one case of wine weighs about 40 pounds), and bottles should be stored on their sides to keep corks moist.

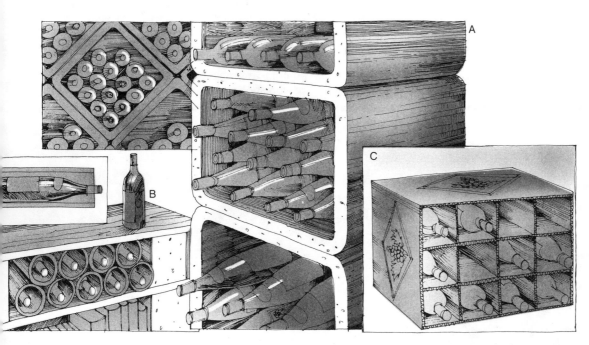

Vintner's classics, easy to re-create

Whether you want storage for a modest supply or a lavish one, these simple ideas may be all you need. Rectangular chimney tiles (A) handle a case or more apiece; round drainpipe tiles or mailing tubes (B) pigeonhole individual bottles. Of course, the simplest solution for short-term storage is to turn a divided cardboard wine box on its side (C).

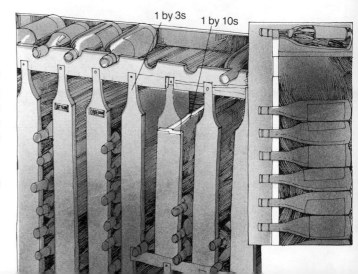

Each slot stacks a case

This stylish vertical slot system is fashioned from vertical 1 by 10s faced with 1 by 3s shaped at the top so that bottles slide up and out. The platform on top displays the contents—up to one case—of each slot below. Make the basic unit 4 feet high; the number of slots is up to you.
Architect: Ron Bogley.

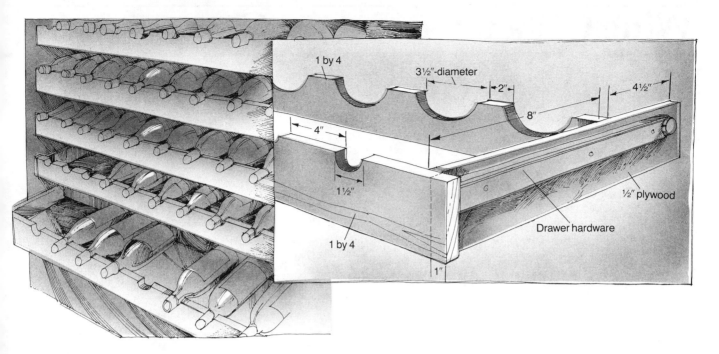

Wine by the drawerful

This handy rack is like a chest of open drawers for wine. To build it, first shape front and rear rails as shown, then connect them with plywood side strips. Mount your new drawers (they shouldn't be more than about 3 feet wide) inside a frame on heavy-duty drawer hardware. The drawers shown are 14 inches deep. Fasten your frame to a wall or to the ceiling for stability. Design: John Hamilton, George Kelce.

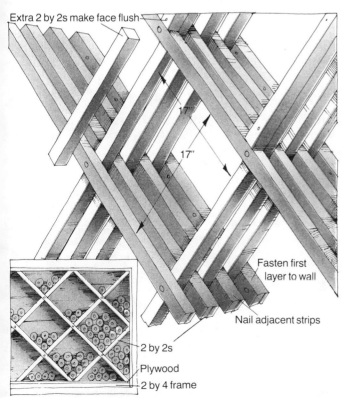

For copious collecting

A large-capacity, diamond-shaped bin system can be built by crisscrossing successive layers of 2 by 2 strips. Rip the 2 by 2s from fir 2 by 4s; seal, stain, and varnish; then assemble. Fasten parallel 2 by 2s to the wall at a 45° angle, as shown (use masonry nails for masonry walls, screws for wood stud walls); then nail on successive layers, each one perpendicular to the last. Eight layers of 2 by 2s provide bins approximately 12 inches deep. To provide additional support for your system, and to keep wines off a damp or dusty floor, position your bins atop a base of 2 by 4s and plywood, as shown.

Your bin system might stretch from wall to wall and from floor to ceiling, but it can be as modest as you like. For a finished look in a smaller unit, enclose the bins within plywood or fir sides and top. The bin size shown holds two cases. Architect: Neil M. Wright.

Wine Cellars for Vintage Care

Why create a wine cellar? For one thing, you'll always have a special bottle on hand when friends drop by. But perhaps more important, by purchasing young wines or sale wines in bulk, then letting them mature in your own cellar, you'll save the appreciable markup that dealers tack on for each year that wines age on *their* shelves. Moreover, many fine wines disappear from the market long before they're mature. A wine cellar or storage area can rapidly save you more money than it cost to build.

Where does a wine cellar go? An attractively finished basement is ideal both for a booming collection and for candlelight tasting parties. But there are other spots—a crawl space (see page 79), a garage corner, an outdoor shed, even an excavated hillside "cave."

Constructing a smaller wine cellar room within a basement or other larger space normally entails building walls, insulating walls and ceiling (see drawing, page 26), then adding racks or bins for wine. A vacant closet or even some unused cabinets form ready-made cellars for small collections.

Regardless of your cellar's size or location, remember four factors for successful wine storage: temperature stability, peace and quiet, absence of light, and bottle positioning.

Temperature: keep it cool and stable

For the optimum aging of wine, it's best to keep your cellar between 50° and 60°F/10° and 16°C; 58°F/14°C is generally regarded as ideal. Some experts, however, wouldn't pale at the idea of storing wines at room temperature — 65° to 70°F/18° to 21°C. Temperature *stability* is more critical than precise temperature: wine can tolerate slow temperature changes over a period of days, but rapid or extreme fluctuations will cause damage.

Insulation is the key to temperature stability. Masonry—the building material for most basements— insulates well. Earth is an excellent natural insulator, which is why so many wine cellars are built below ground level. You don't have a basement? Search the house for an area that stays naturally cool (the north side of the house is shadiest) or that can be vented to a naturally cool crawl space or outside area.

Your cellar should not be near the furnace, heating ducts, or water heater. Insulating the walls heavily (the more the better) will stabilize temperatures. And don't forget the door — it should be solid-core with double weatherstripping. In cool climates, you can leave cool (usually north or east) basement walls uninsulated. Where it's warm, you might choose a power fan or air conditioning unit with an automatic thermostat to keep the wine cool. Though it does consume energy, an air conditioner might be needed only two to three months a year if the cellar is well insulated, and it needn't be overly powerful. Cellar humidity, although not critical, is best around 50 percent. If your cellar is too damp, the labels may fall off your bottles — resulting in a real guessing game.

Peace and quiet

The conditions required for storing wines may sound like a sickroom atmosphere, but wine should not be disturbed. Protect it from sources of vibration such as stairways, washers, and dryers. Sturdy wine racks will help (see pages 56–57); in earthquake country, bolt your racks to fixed walls.

Shut out the light

Direct sunlight and other sources of ultraviolet light may harm wines (specifically, the yeast organisms still alive within the bottle), so make your cellar lightproof. But don't forget good artificial light for those times when you're hunting for that special bottle or hosting a wine-tasting party.

Keep bottles on their sides

Efficient wine racks are the key to organizing your cellar space. For specifics on racks, see pages 56–57. A genuine cork is the traditional sign that a bottle of wine deserves special care. The cork breathes slightly, so it must be kept moist by the wine inside to prevent air or airborne organisms from entering and spoiling the wine.

Store bottles on their sides or at a slight tilt from the horizontal, with necks toward you for easy access. To help sort out the Beaujolais from the Zinfandel, hang small labels around the necks, or label each slot in your rack. Keep a complete log of all your wines and their locations.

A simple corner cellar

Wooden grid panels, fore and aft, allow prize wines to rest at their preferred angle. Counter is handy for uncorking bottles and pouring wine. Architect: Kenneth Lim.

Elegant enough for entertaining

This wine cellar is much more than a wine storage room—the owners enjoy their converted crawl space so much that they have dinner parties here. From the table, guests can admire the triangular wine bins, each of which holds about a case of wine. A serving alcove in the wall opposite the bins is fitted with a rack for wine glasses. The brick floor and rough redwood paneling add to the atmosphere and help insulate the cellar. Design: Jean Chappell.

Garages,
Attics &
Basements

Turning troublesome spaces into work-for-you places

Closet within a closet *takes advantage of normally wasted space along attic eaves. The small access door opens from the master bedroom closet. Architect: James Jessup.*

Space below the basement stairs *is fitted with shelves and hooks; floor space is open for bulky items.*

Garage corner *lends plenty of wall space for bicycles, hand tools, and camping gear. The cutaway workbench with shelves underneath is a bonus. Architect: Wendell H. Lovett.*

Garages

Maximizing storage, yet leaving space for the car

A loft for lightweight items, *simple racks for tools, and roomy utility shelves help organize this garage. All of these features stretch storage space even when the car's inside. The tool rack is made from 1 by 4 rails fastened to studs. For loft-building help, see page 65. Design: Steve Wolgemuth.*

You can't find your best pair of hedge clippers. Ah!—you spy them hanging on a nail in the corner of what has become a jungle—the garage. Up, down, and around you go, clearing a path to the corner. As you balance among a garden rake, birdcage, mattress frame, and broken lawn chair, reaching for the clippers, you stumble and fall onto a pile of laundry next to the washing machine. The clippers are still in the corner.

Clearly, you're out of storage space in your garage or carport, and it's time to do something about it. Consider organizing your belongings, improving your present storage facilities and adding new ones, or extending the building.

As you tackle your garage storage problems, think "clean up and look up"—this can be your byword for discovering and using your garage's storage potential. A thorough cleanup alone can drastically increase your garage's capacity. And once your belongings are sorted through, you'll be able to make better use of existing and added storage units such as shelves, drawers, pegboards, and roll-outs.

But don't forget to look up. Overhead storage —cabinets, platforms, lofts, and ledges—can be used to tame your garage jungle and create room for a much needed laundry center, workshop, or potting table. Overhead storage is also feasible in carports, which call for secure, weatherproof storage units.

If you're already organized, this section will show you how to improve your garage—and the time you spend in it—with better heating, lighting, ventilation, and other amenities. And if you can't possibly fit in another paint can or tricycle, you'll find some ideas here on how to increase storage space by extending the garage itself.

Your garage's or carport's storage potential

With building costs multiplying as quickly as your storage inventory, you may well turn to your existing garage or carport with fresh hopes. Its length and width determine the structure's basic amount of available space, of course, but other factors count, too. Here are some questions to consider: How high is the roof? Is it flat or peaked? How large is your car? Does it need year-round protection?

Garage dimensions. Garages are nominally termed "one-car," "two-car," and "three-car." The size of a one-car garage begins at about 10 feet by 20 feet—small, but you can probably squeeze some good storage space out of it. You're in luck if your one-car garage has a peaked roof. Two-car spaces run upward from 8½ feet by 20 feet; 25 feet square is ideal. If you have a three-car space, you have a head start on storage.

Garage and carport types. The design of your garage or carport affects its storage potential. Garage walls are usually built from wood framing and sheathing, cement blocks, or prefabricated metal panels. Building materials have little influence on storage capacity, but it's easier to attach storage units to wood frame walls than to masonry or metal. Wood frame walls also allow shallow storage between studs.

A carport's open structure is a different story. Because carport storage is more exposed to weather and theft, you'll want to limit storage of valuables to lockable weatherproof units; install them either along the carport's perimeter or overhead.

Gable and hip roofs (see drawing below) are tops for storage. Shed-roof structures also provide some overhead space between the rafters and ceiling line. In a flat-roofed garage, you're limited to the space between the top of your head or vehicle and the ceiling.

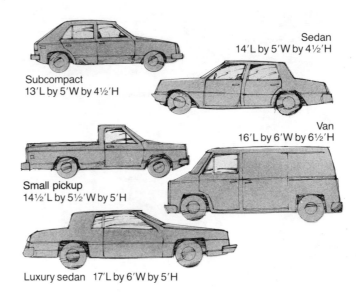

Subcompact 13'L by 5'W by 4½'H

Sedan 14'L by 5'W by 4½'H

Van 16'L by 6'W by 6½'H

Small pickup 14½'L by 5½'W by 5'H

Luxury sedan 17'L by 6'W by 5'H

your storage plans to the size of your vehicle or vehicles, but keep in mind that some day you might want to sell your home to a family with two vans.

Clearance. In your garage or carport, clearance is the space needed around the car when the car is parked inside; it affects how much room you'll have to work with when planning where to put storage units, appliances, and worktables.

See the drawing below for minimum clearance recommendations around typical vehicles. To calculate how much storage space you have to work with, drive your vehicle or vehicles into place. Then measure the distance from each vehicle to the ceiling, walls, rafters, and other obstructions. Subtract the recommended clearance figures, and you have the bottom line—the real storage potential.

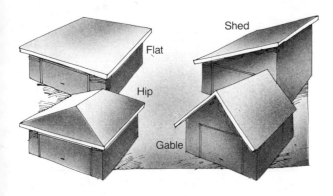

Flat

Shed

Hip

Gable

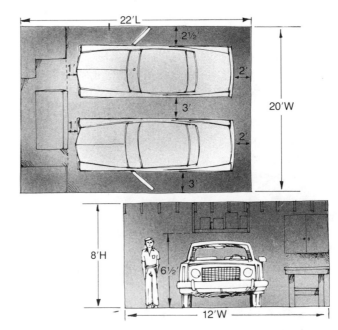

22'L · 2½' · 1' · 2' · 3' · 1' · 2' · 3' · 20'W

8'H · 6½' · 12'W

Subcompacts and limousines. The sizes of your automobiles directly affect the available floor space in a garage or carport. Fortunately for the storage-needy, average car dimensions have been shrinking (see drawing at right above for sample dimensions). Adapt

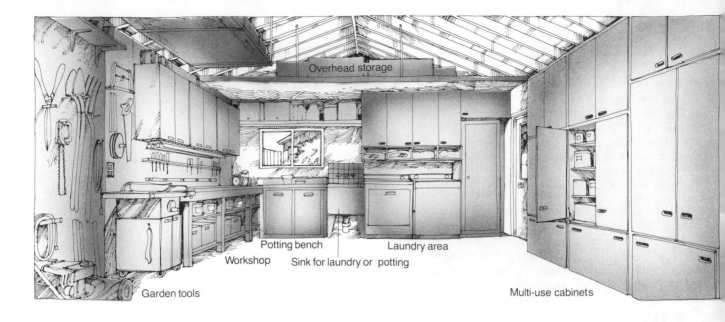

Overhead storage

Potting bench

Workshop   Sink for laundry or potting   Laundry area

Garden tools   Multi-use cabinets

The multi-use garage and carport

After you've assessed your usable storage space, take stock of what you need to store. Do you want to make room for that laundry center, workshop, or potting bench? Efficient overall planning, plus storage units especially designed for your garage or carport, will open up more space than you might imagine.

Coordinating your garage layout

The keys to an efficient garage layout are 1) using all available space, leaving minimum clearances next to, behind, and above vehicles; and 2) grouping items that go together—gardening supplies, for example.

Because most storage problems stem from a lack of floor space, you'll do well to raise storage units above the ground whenever possible. You can hang them high on a wall or suspend them from the joists or rafters. Or you can build an "upstairs" loft.

The items you use most often should, of course, be close at hand. Awkward spots and places that are inaccessible when the car is inside (such as rafter space) are best for seasonal or long-term storage.

Plan hanging shelves or wall-mounted cabinets around the contour of your car's hood and roof (see clearance diagram, preceding page). To ensure safe parking, attach a tennis ball to a cord with a fishhook or eyescrew, and hang the ball so that it will nudge your windshield when the car is properly parked; or fasten a length of 4 by 4 to the garage slab to "curb" the front wheels when the car is in place.

Some garage work areas to consider include these: a laundry center with sink and cabinets (see pages 38–39); a home workshop, with places for hand and power tools (pages 52–55); a house maintenance center for paint brushes, spare plumbing and electrical parts,

brooms, solvents, and cleaners; a potting center with workbench, mounted cabinets, and tilt-out bins; a garden maintenance area where you can gather such tools as the lawn mower, rake, clippers, and weeders; and a mudroom and closet for boots, rain gear, and other outdoor or seasonal clothes (see pages 20–23).

Position such areas for convenience and good working conditions. An outdoor maintenance area, for example, should be handy to the garden or yard.

Storage units for the garage

Here's a brief guide to storage units particularly suited for the garage (see drawing on facing page).

Between-stud shelves. Most garage walls are of wood frame construction; the vertical studs are spaced 16 or 24 inches apart, center to center. The shallow, uniform area between studs is ideal for storing miscellaneous small items like nail jars, engine oil, and paint cans.

Open shelves. Build freestanding frames for shelves or hang shelf units (those with backs) from the wall. You can also use adjustable tracks and brackets, L-braces, individual brackets, or continuous brackets attached to studs to hold up shelves. If your garage walls are of brick or concrete block, back shelves against the wall, hang them from ceiling joists, or use special masonry fasteners (see pages 78–79 for types and installation tips).

Cabinets, drawers, and closets. Enclosed units keep dust and moisture out, and help to organize easily lost small items. Large tools, lawn mowers, and cleaning supplies fit into vertical closets. Recycled cabinets from a remodeled kitchen are perfect for the garage. Securely locked, enclosed units keep children safe from garden poisons and sharp tools, and guard against theft. Sliding doors, roll-down window shades, or tilt-out bins make large units more accessible in tight places. For more on cabinets, see page 10.

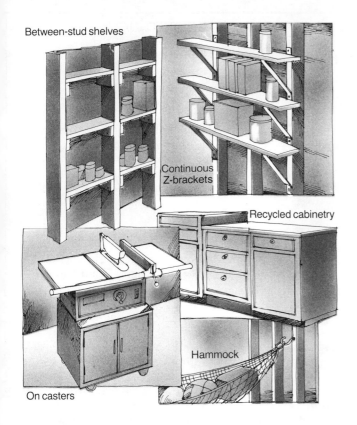

Between-stud shelves

Continuous
Z-brackets

Recycled cabinetry

On casters

Hammock

Racks and pegs. Most versatile for hanging storage is the pegboard hanger system shown on page 7. Oversize carpenter's nails and spikes, or dowels set into wall studs, can hold garden chairs—even ladders. Commercially manufactured racks, whether of heavy-duty metal or vinyl-coated wire, are versatile but more costly.

Roll-outs. One way to fit storage units, workbenches, or equipment into a tight garage is to mount them on heavy-duty casters. Store them close to the wall, then roll them out onto the main floor when the car is out.

Overhead storage units. Even in flat-roofed garages, overhead joists—the horizontal cousins of wall studs—form cubbyholes that are great for small storage, especially for seasonal or infrequently used items. To provide easy overhead "shelving," nail boards across joist bottoms (use heavy nails). A nylon or canvas hammock draped above head level can be used to store lightweight items such as seasonal sports equipment and winter blankets.

Overhead platforms

Often the most neglected storage space throughout a house is the area above your head. Garages with gable, hip, or shed roofs are ideal for anything from a perimeter ledge (page 41) to a finished upstairs room.

When putting overhead garage space to work, remember to leave adequate clearance for the garage door to operate smoothly—and for you and your family to move freely about the garage. In general, any

loft or other overhead structure that you'll be walking under should be at least 6½ feet above the ground.

Building a loft. An overhead loft is an effective means to increasing storage space—especially in a cramped one-car garage—and it's comparatively straightforward for you and a helper to build. To construct the simplest type of loft, take advantage of existing ceiling joists, adding more joists as necessary. Lay a ½ or ⅝-inch plywood "floor" on top of the joists (use ⅝-inch sheets if you're going to be using the loft for heavy storage).

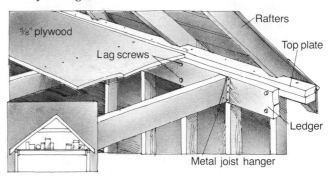

⅝" plywood

Rafters

Top plate

Lag screws

Ledger

Metal joist hanger

When planning a garage loft, inspect the size and condition of the existing joists. High-quality 2 by 6s should be strong enough to support the weight of ordinary storage. But if you plan to walk on the surface or store heavy furniture in the loft, or if the joists must span more than 12 feet, they should be stouter than 2 by 6s. Diagonal 1 by 4 braces running between joists and overhead rafters provide extra support. Ask your local building department about requirements in your area. Joists should be spaced on 16-inch centers for heavy storage.

If you have to add ceiling joists, remember that ideally they should sit on opposing top plates. If the top plates are inaccessible, bolt ledger strips to the wall studs, attach metal joist hangers, and use these to support the joists.

With a peaked roof framed by trusses (see drawing on page 70) or low collar beams, install smaller plywood platforms in the spaces between consecutive trusses (commonly 24 inches) or beams; support the platforms with 2 by 4 cleats nailed to the sides of the trusses.

Access. To gain access to your new loft, use a sturdy stepladder or utility ladder. For a large loft space, see page 73 for information on building stairs and other kinds of access. If you plan to haul bulky, heavy items up and down, a narrow ladder is not only exasperating, but also dangerous.

Pulley system. You might consider a suspended plywood platform operated with pulleys (see page 41) for garage storage. Here's another option: bend 1-inch-wide iron straps so that they extend 3 inches under the platform on each side, and screw them to the bottom and sides. Attach cable or rope to the strap ends. This kind of unit should be used for lightweight storage only.

Carport storage ideas

The two major shortcomings of carport storage are exposure to weather and lack of security; the most common solution to both is to install enclosed cabinets. Build units from exterior-grade ¾-inch plywood, and finish them with tough exterior enamel or polyurethane. (See page 10 for more details on cabinets.) Build units with bases that raise them several inches above the floor; either waterproof the bases or build them with pressure-treated lumber. For greater security, use good locks and hasps (see page 10) and inside-mounted hinges.

The number one spot for carport storage units is between the roof support posts. Attach units to the floor slab, suspend them from overhead beams, or add intermediate vertical framing to hold them up. A long cabinet might have separate doored compartments—one shelved, one with drawers, and one without interior divisions. Units that have doors that slide or that open to the outside leave more clearance inside the carport (see drawing on page 63 for minimum clearances).

If your carport has a pitched gable or hip roof, consider an overhead storage area (see page 65). Lockable plywood chests bolted to a loft "floor," joists, or ledger strips can be used to store valuables (see drawing below).

A small room—perhaps 6 feet by 8 feet—added to the rear of the carport and equipped with windows, electrical outlets, and a small heater, makes a protected "mini-workshop," laundry, or crafts studio. You can fit such a room with shelves, pegboard, and other open storage standbys.

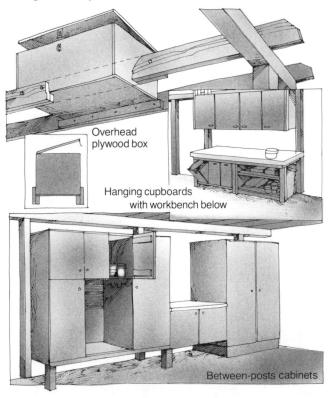

Overhead plywood box

Hanging cupboards with workbench below

Between-posts cabinets

Garage improvements

If your garage (or carport) is to be used for more than parking, it may require specific improvements to ensure that it's safe, comfortable for working, weathertight, and up to code. Consider these possibilities:

Ventilation. To prevent the buildup of moisture, auto exhaust, paint fumes, or shop dust in a closed garage, open ventilation is a necessity. As a rule, there should be 1 square foot of open vent space per 150 square feet of floor area. A laundry must have its own vent system.

Insulation. You might choose to insulate your garage for either of two reasons: 1) to prevent swings in temperature that might damage storage; or 2) to make a heated garage more energy efficient. Put insulation between wall studs and rafters. Choose fiberglass batts, blankets, or rigid board insulation with a vapor barrier, or add a plastic barrier (see pages 70–71).

Lighting. Ideally, you should mix natural and artificial light. To obtain more natural light, install windows and skylights, or replace a large section of a wall, or even the garage door, with translucent panels. Carports are often roofed with rippled plastic sheeting that lets in muted light. By placing garage windows high, you'll save wall space for storage.

Overhead fluorescent shop units are the most efficient for general artificial lighting; one 4-foot double-tube shop unit lights up about 40 square feet. Place individual, adjustable spotlights—incandescent or fluorescent—where direct lighting is needed. Paint the garage walls and ceiling, as well as pegboard storage panels, white to amplify light by reflection.

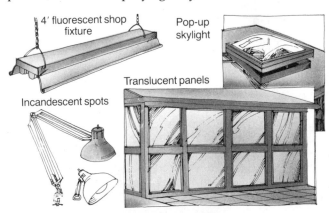

4' fluorescent shop fixture

Pop-up skylight

Translucent panels

Incandescent spots

Wiring. Power tools and garage lighting should be on different circuits; a tool or laundry circuit should be at least 20 amps. Install as many circuits as possible to prevent an overload. A laundry, a workshop, or an electric heater may require up to 240 volts.

Several grounded (three-prong) electrical outlets are a necessity, and continuous power strips are a great convenience. You can run wires either underground or overhead from a power source to a detached garage.

Plumbing. Laundries, photo darkrooms, garden center sinks, hose spigots, and mudrooms may require plumbing improvements. Extending plumbing to a detached garage can be a problem. Remember that outdoor pipes must be placed below the frost line (check local codes), and facilities that require plumbing must be higher than the drainage system. In freezing climates, plumbing systems for unheated garages or carports should be equipped with shutoff valves.

Floors. Concrete slab floors are standard. If you want to use your garage for work or play during the day and for car storage at night, you can protect the floor from oil drippings by laying down a 10-mil layer of polyethylene sheeting. For a more finished look, you might consider vinyl-asbestos tiles; some types take wear and tear from cars surprisingly well.

To insulate and dress up a drab slab, simply cover the floor with straw mats or colorful rugs. You can also paint the slab with special concrete paint, or lay vinyl-asbestos or asphalt tiles in adhesive over the concrete (waterproof it first). If you want to use a covering that requires a wooden base, you can build up such a base over the waterproofed concrete (see pages 78–79 for details). A separate work area within your garage or carport might warrant such treatment.

Heating. Insulation and a built-up subfloor in the work area will help reduce heat loss. To provide heat, you have three options: 1) extend ducts from your central heating system to the garage (not feasible with detached garages); 2) install a separate forced-air unit in the garage (illegal in some areas); or 3) set up a built-in or portable room heater—probably your best choice.

The four types of room heaters are these: electric (baseboard, portable, or quartz type); kerosene; oil or gas wall heaters (designed to fit between wall studs); and woodstoves. Neither a kerosene heater nor a woodstove requires any power hookup, but both need ventilation; a woodstove also requires special fittings and flashing.

Room heaters operate either by convection (they heat the air in a room) or by radiation (they heat objects first). Radiation is most effective in a small area. In general, wall-mounted units are more efficient, but a portable unit can go where you go.

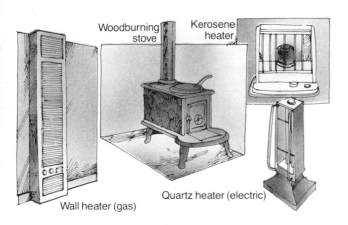

Wall heater (gas) Woodburning stove Kerosene heater Quartz heater (electric)

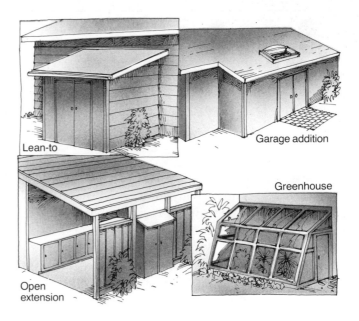

Lean-to Garage addition Greenhouse Open extension

Garage extensions

You've tried all the possibilities, but you just can't fit all your sports gear, garden tools, and lumber into the garage. Before you build a new structure—shed, carport, or garage—consider a simpler garage extension.

Extension types. An extension represents a smaller investment in both time and money than a new structure, and takes less space. Among your options (see drawing above): a roof extension for sheltering a car, boat, or RV—or for storage and work space in milder climates; a lean-to with outside access; a glass greenhouse version of the lean-to (consider a prefabricated unit); or a garage addition. If you're ambitious, you can also convert a one-car to a two-car garage.

Building tips. An extension borrows the garage's framework for part of its structural support. A lean-to is essentially three walls and a roof—the fourth wall is the garage. More elaborate additions entail cutting a door between the garage and an added room, or "punching out" an entire wall. In such cases, be sure to preserve adequate structural supports (headers) for the remaining garage framework. When any structural alterations are required, consult a contractor or architect for recommendations, and have your plans checked out by local building inspectors. Building codes may place limits on extension materials, height, setback from the property line, and foundation type.

Normally, an extension is built over a poured concrete slab that has been tied into the garage slab. However, a more solid foundation, extending below the frost line, may be required in severe climates. Your new extension must be weathertight: provide a sound roof and install flashing where the extension adjoins the old garage roof or siding. Select a design, materials, and colors that match or complement your garage and house.

Attics

Taking the mystery out of access, sloping walls, air vents, and floors

An attic is like a treasure chest—it's usually filled with a few treasures, some disappointments, and a little mystery. Grandfather's steamer trunk, your summer camping gear, and holiday decorations are your treasures. But how do you take the mystery out of storing—and finding—prize possessions within that oddly shaped space?

Attics are scarce in modern housing, particularly in the West. If you grew up with an attic or recently acquired an older or custom home with an attic, you'll welcome solutions to the storage problems posed by attics. These pages offer ways to create a great storage area that's warm, dry, accessible, and even pleasant to visit.

Even if you don't have a formal attic, you may still have a low crawl space above the ceiling that you can convert into a handy storage area.

These are the biggest problems confronting those who wish to make good use of attic space: the awkwardness of sloping walls, sharp roof peaks, and unfinished floors; temperature fluctuations—stifling heat in the summer and icy air in the winter; dampness and humidity from roof leaks and improper air circulation; and insufficient access from below. The following sections treat these problems individually. Overcoming them is something many homeowners can do themselves; refer to the *Sunset* book *Basic Carpentry Illustrated*.

Anatomy of an attic. *The classic attic triangle is shaped by opposing roof rafters rising to a ridge board at the peak, and by floor joists—which double as ceiling joists downstairs—that span the outer house walls. Collar beams sometimes brace opposing rafters, or are added as ceiling supports. Plywood sheets or "1-by" strip boards laid atop the joists serve as flooring. In addition to the open floor space, use these three key storage areas: along the sloping walls, against the gable walls, and along the ridge line.*

An attic overview

An attic's shape—and its capacity for storage—depend on how steeply the roof is pitched (attic height) and on the house's dimensions (floor space). Steep roofs make the best attics, flat roofs none at all. For a living space, a room should normally have a 7½-foot ceiling over at least one-half of the available floor space. For storage, though, you can use whatever space is accessible. Even a minimal crawl space, common in newer homes, has usable storage space.

Organizing your attic

Familiarize yourself with the attic vocabulary explained in the drawing on the facing page. Then add two more terms: *organization* and *accessibility*.

An attic's layout needn't be stylish or fancy, but it should be orderly. The goal is to organize the attic so that you can easily find everything. Arrange related objects in one place, and store those you use often where they're easy to reach. To save a lot of teeth-gnashing, label covered items and boxes with permanent ink on white tape for identification, and keep an inventory of everything in the attic.

Those small, fragile keepsakes requiring extra protection from moisture, dust, and insects should be carefully packed in sturdy boxes and sealed; cover furniture with mattress pads and wrap with polyethylene.

Fitting storage to the attic

An attic's configuration is usually a challenge for orderly storage. How do you deal with sloping walls, corners you have to crawl into, triangular gable walls, and the high but narrow ridge line overhead? Here are some tested ideas; see pages 6–11, too, for general information on storage units.

Sloping walls. You can either shape storage units to conform to eave spaces or give up on the eaves and build vertical units. A 4-foot-high knee wall unit with cabinet doors, recessed drawers, or even a curtain across the front is an efficient way to use eave space (see drawing below). Knee wall units should not be deeper than your reach, unless they're large enough to be walk-ins.

Simpler solutions? Shelves hung with rope or chain, or items hanging from a closet rod, use the force of gravity to square off attic space. Or between adjacent rafters, horizontal 1 by 12s create another version of "between-stud" shelves for out-of-the-way storage.

Gable walls are good spots for a combination closet to store seasonal clothes, toys, and sporting goods. Shelves are easy to fit on a gable wall: install track and bracket hardware for shelves (see drawing below), or place shelves or cabinets along the base of the wall.

Articles that would be damaged by extremes of heat or cold (artwork, for example) shouldn't be stored against a gable wall unless it's insulated. This is particularly true if the gable wall is on the north side of the house or if it's exposed to direct sun for substantial periods. Also, be sure not to block any vents in the wall (page 71).

Along the ridge line. Cut off the triangular peak with rope-hung or chain-hung shelves (accessible from the sides), or hang storage from long nails, hooks, and pegs fixed high on the rafters. A closet rod or simply a long 1 by 2 fastened to opposing rafters will support garment bags full of seasonal clothes. If there's a ridge vent (page 71), don't block it.

To form an "attic within an attic"—a scaled-down version of the loft platform on page 65—place boards or plywood between existing collar beams or between beams you've added yourself. Such a platform should be used for lightweight storage only.

Sloping walls

Gable walls

Ridge line

Cramped quarters. Many newer homes, particularly in the West and South, were built with relatively flat roofs that leave only a minimal attic or a crawl space. Usually, even a crawl space has some usable storage in the middle and at the gable ends. You can at least lay down plywood around the access hatch. If you can reach the gables easily, build storage cupboards and a catwalk (page 72) leading from the hatch.

Truss framing presents an obstacle to increased attic use; the trusses integrate rafters, collar beams, and sometimes ceiling joists into single framing members, usually spaced 24 inches apart. Trusses may not be removed or cut into, so storage must be built around or between them. Access will often be a trial, as you have to crawl through the spaces within trusses. But don't give up—lay down plywood (see below) and make the most of the space.

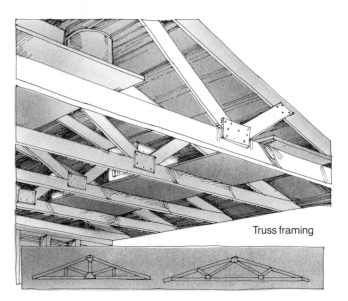

Truss framing

Solving attic problems

Attics revive that old cliché "Out of sight, out of mind." Often you won't notice an attic's problems until you open up the space for storables that demand dry, stable conditions.

Your major enemies are swings in temperature and moisture. If the space is improperly vented or insulated, an attic's temperature might soar to 150° in August, then plunge below freezing in January. Moisture enters the picture as humidity from downstairs condenses on cold attic walls, or—more trying—through a roof leak (for information on making repairs, see the *Sunset* book *Roofing & Siding)*.

To eliminate swings in temperature, install insulation between the roof rafters and along gable walls. Add a vapor barrier to prevent humid house air from condensing inside the attic. To improve ventilation, consider adding gable vents, soffit vents, ridge vents, turbine vents, and fans.

Attic insulation—the "balancer"

Insulation slows the transfer of heat from one space to another through a solid surface—wall, roof, or floor. Attic insulation is a "balancer"—it prevents warm air from escaping through the roof in winter, and slows down the accumulation of heat from outside in summer. An "R-rating" is given to all standard building materials—the higher the number, the more effective the insulation.

How much insulation does your attic need? Climate and personal choice are factors: check with the building department for the optimum R-rating where you live.

Where does it go? To make an attic suitable for storage or living space, insulation should be placed between the roof rafters and used to line gable walls—not incorporated into the attic floor as is common. You could insulate behind knee walls—ending the storage space there—instead of the lowest rafters. If your attic floor, or the ceiling below, is already insulated, so much the better; such insulation slows down humidity and heat exchange and deadens sound.

Insulation types. In unfinished attics the most common types of insulation are blankets or batts of spun fiberglass or rock wool, and lightweight rigid boards of compressed fiberglass, polystyrene, or urethane. Blankets and batts are sized to fit common framing gaps of 22½ inches and 14½ inches. Panels are available in the following sizes: 4 feet by 8 feet, 4 feet by 4 feet, and 2 feet by 8 feet. Different thicknesses have different R-ratings. Blankets are easier to install, but boards have a higher R-rating per inch of thickness. Some codes require that insulation be covered with ½-inch gypsum wallboard or a layer of another fire-retardant material.

Vapor barriers. It's necessary in all but the driest climates to install a vapor barrier to prevent humid house air from condensing inside attic walls and roof materials. Blankets and batts are commonly sold with a vapor barrier of foil or kraft paper; if your insulation doesn't have this protection, cover it with polyethylene sheeting (at least 2 mils thick), foil-backed wallboard, or asphalt-covered building paper. Normally, vapor barriers should face in toward the attic.

Attic ventilation

For a simple solution to heat buildup in summer, and humidity and condensation in the winter, try good ventilation. *Natural ventilation* takes advantage of thermal air movement and wind pressure; *power ventilation* uses an electric fan to push or draw hot air up and out of the attic through vents near the ridge line.

The key to proper ventilation is the placement of the vents. The lower drawing on the facing page illustrates the various options for placing vents—but you won't need all those vents. You'll need about 1 square foot of

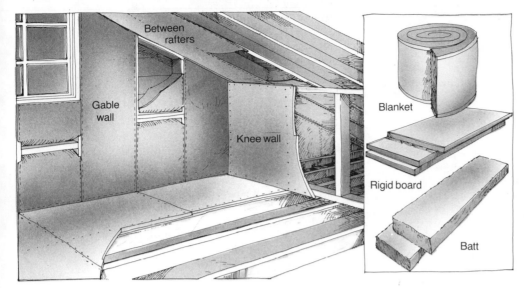

Between rafters

Gable wall

Knee wall

Blanket

Rigid board

Batt

Insulate the shell. *If you're developing attic storage or workspace, provide attic insulation between rafters and inside gable walls. Check your building department for the optimum local "R-rating," then choose from blankets, batts, or rigid boards. Buy insulation with an attached vapor barrier, or add polyethylene sheeting—2-mil or thicker. (The vapor barrier faces inside.) Cover insulation with fire-retardant wallboard or paneling.*

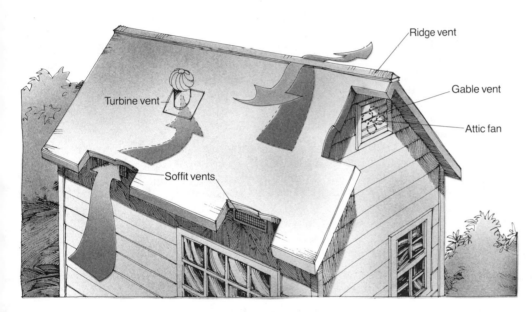

Ridge vent

Gable vent

Attic fan

Turbine vent

Soffit vents

Attic ventilation. *Natural air movement is the key to attic vent placement. Cooler air enters low, pushing rising hot air out the top. Low soffit vents coupled with ridge or gable vents are standard. For problem cases, an electric fan in a downwind gable expels hot air quickly. Slotted turbine vents set up a natural vacuum when the wind blows.*

open vent space (don't count screens or slats) per 150 square feet of floor area.

Gable vents are set in the gable walls, as close to the ridge line as possible. They're usually installed in pairs: one facing into the prevailing wind, the other downwind. A breeze entering one vent pushes hot attic air out the other. Gable vents are often combined with soffit vents. To prevent icy winds from blowing through your attic, close or cover a windward vent during the winter.

Soffit (eave) vents are openings at the attic floor level, below the rafter overhang, that bring cool air into the attic. This air is drawn up by warm-air convection, which forces hot air out vents near the ridge line.

Ridge vents are very efficient, but they're troublesome to install. They release hot air from the roof peak, and

because they're two-sided, they'll always vent in the downwind direction. Ridge vents require extensive complementary soffit venting below for good results.

Turbine vents. When the wind is blowing, the slotted ball atop the vent rotates freely, creating a vacuum that draws attic air up and out. The vent remains open when the wind doesn't blow.

Electric attic fans are powerful tools for pushing hot air out of an attic. A fan is inserted into a cutout in the gable wall, then wired; it's usually paired with an opening in the attic floor that draws air from the house below. Some fans are equipped with a thermostat that conveniently monitors their operation. The disadvantages of electric fans—aside from the effort it takes to install them—are that they consume energy and make noise; some fire codes prohibit their use (see page 49).

Upgrading your attic

If your attic is properly insulated and ventilated, you're ready to attend to three other big considerations: your attic's floor, lighting, and accessibility.

The attic floor

Is your attic floor ready for storage or heavy traffic? If the floor joists are exposed, the answer is a loud "no." *Don't* walk or place storage in the areas between joists—that's your downstairs ceiling, not intended to support weight. For flooring, you can choose between an attic "catwalk" and a finished floor.

A catwalk is a narrow weight-bearing surface extending the length of the attic and possibly to areas under the eaves. With a catwalk you can gain access to the whole attic area without balancing on joists or installing a complete floor.

A catwalk—or a portion of one—is usually built of plywood laid right on top of the joists. Be sure the joists are strong enough—see "A new attic floor," below. Standard plywood sheets ⅝-inch thick are usually adequate, provided you can fit the large (4 feet by 8 feet) sheets up into the attic. If you can't fit standard plywood sheets through the hatch, the stairway, or a dormer opening, cut the sheets down to a manageable size or use strip lumber (1 by 6s should be adequate).

A new attic floor. Attic floor joists, which are of course also the ceiling joists for downstairs, may not be built to support the weight of human traffic, heavy storage,

or furniture. Your first task is to inspect the joists. Check two things: the spacing of the joists—which should be 16 inches center to center (or 24 inches if the joists are stout enough); and the joist dimensions—joists should be at least 2 by 8s for heavy use, even more stout for long spans. Check with building department officials for requirements in your area.

See the drawing below for details about installing new joists, if necessary, and laying a floor. About floors: for simple utility and strength, ⅝-inch or ¾-inch plywood is the best choice. Plywood is easy to lay, adds rigidity and strength to the floor structure, and is usually squeakproof. Top-grade plywood isn't necessary for attic floors. However, special subfloor panels with tongue-and-groove edges are stronger than standard plywood, though they cost more.

Lighting

Light fixtures don't have to be fancy in the attic, but they should provide illumination where it's most needed. Well-placed electric lights can save you a lot of anguish when you're looking for small items under the eaves or atop a ridge line shelf. One main attic light should be operable from a switch below; individual lights can be turned on by switches or pullchains as you move about the attic.

Attic access

Is your attic readily accessible? How do you plan to use it? If it's for light or seasonal storage only—especially in minimal crawl spaces—a trap door and folding ladder will probably be adequate. Heavier storage requires

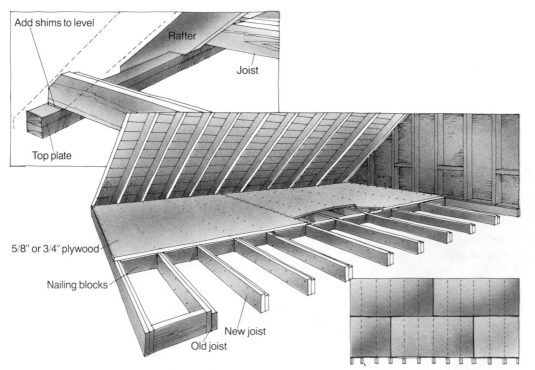

Add shims to level

Rafter

Joist

Top plate

5/8" or 3/4" plywood

Nailing blocks

New joist

Old joist

Laying a floor. *If your present joists aren't up to the task of supporting stored items, you'll have to add new ones. Lay new joists next to old ones (if the original spacing is correct); nail the new joists to the old and to the top plate or bearing wall at each end. To level the new joists, slip small wood blocks or shims beneath them as necessary.*

Then it's on to the plywood floor. Lay the sheets lengthwise across the joists; panel ends should meet midway over a joist for solid support. Stagger rows so that no two adjacent joints line up. Adding nailing blocks between joists or installing tongue-and-groove plywood strengthens edges

a sturdy ladder or stairs, as well as a larger opening for lugging mattresses, dressers, and chairs up and in. If you'll be using the space frequently, you'll almost certainly want a fixed stairway.

Stairs or ladders adjoining a wall will be sturdier, safer, and less obtrusive than those placed further out in a room. Remember, though, that stairways are often required by code to have a minimum of 6½ feet of headroom, so a stair opening in the attic can't be tucked under the eaves.

The access opening. Here are the three rules for an attic opening: 1) the opening must be large enough for you and your storage to fit through without undue gymnastics; 2) you should have sufficient overhead clearance when you step up into the attic; and 3) the ladder or stairway should not interfere with traffic patterns or take up too much space below.

A door-size opening will admit most large storage. Width is the critical dimension, though. Homeowners with limited crawl spaces can make do with a push-up hatch smaller than door size.

Look for ways to provide attic access from out-of-the-way spots. If your garage is attached, you may be able to get into the attic from the garage. You could also remove the ceiling from a large closet, install a ladder, and convert a crawl space above into a "storage loft."

Ladders—fixed and fold-down. Fixed ladders and fold-down stairs are best for occasional traffic and light storage. Fold-down stairs, available from building suppliers or well-stocked hardware stores, swing up into the ceiling to close, leaving open floor space below; they also demand little clearance above. Their disadvantages: they usually provide no hand support and they lack stability. Look for a ladder with minimal bounce at the hinges.

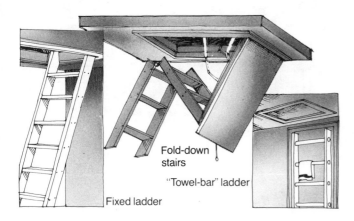

Fold-down stairs

"Towel-bar" ladder

Fixed ladder

Fixed ladders are more stable, especially when fastened to a wall. They range from traditional structures to door-mounted rungs that double as towel bars (see drawing above). In general, the heavier the intended use, the more sturdy the ladder should be. A ladder's biggest drawback is its steepness; it's difficult to climb up and down with full hands.

Planning your staircase. A well-crafted main staircase is a carpenter's showpiece, demanding the same attention to detail as fine cabinetry. But, an unadorned flight of attic utility stairs is much easier to build than it may look, and it doesn't require fancy materials or many tools. The key is in the planning.

First, consider your available space and the total rise and total run to be covered; then choose your basic stair type and dimensions accordingly. The three basic types, as shown below, are straight-run, "L"-type, and "U"-type. Straight-run stairs are the easiest and cheapest to build; L and U-types are better in tight spaces and for avoiding obstructions. Spiral or "winder" stairs, a fourth type, take up even less space, but they're awkward and dangerous for transporting storage goods up and down; some local codes ban their use altogether.

A typical stair assembly consists of stringers, risers, treads, and railings. Design factors, which are commonly subject to building codes, include riser height, tread depth, stair angle, and stair width. The drawing below illustrates the major elements. Check local codes for specific requirements in your area.

Stairways may be open or closed, or a combination of the two. Open sides should be equipped with handrails above vertical banisters or a solid side guard. On a closed side, a rail can be wall-mounted with metal brackets. Manufactured assemblies are common, but a 2 by 4 rail and supports are sufficient.

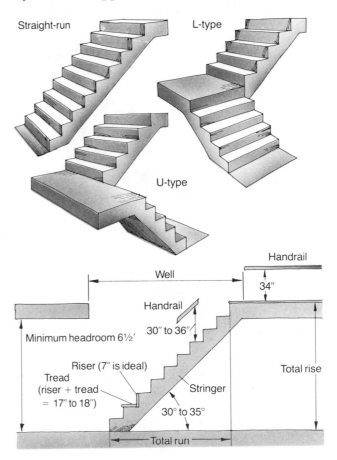

Straight-run

L-type

U-type

Handrail

Well

34"

Handrail

30" to 36"

Minimum headroom 6½'

Riser (7" is ideal)

Tread
(riser + tread = 17" to 18")

Stringer

Total rise

30° to 35°

Total run

Basements

Getting on top of what's down under: ideas for dry storage

Like the Rock of Gibraltar, a basement should be an impregnable fortress, impervious to weather, water, and rodents. If your fortress is crumbling under the attack of any or all of these enemies, you're probably wondering how to guard your storage.

In the following pages, we show you how to solve moisture problems, whether from sweating pipes or outright leaks, and how to control basement temperatures by using insulation, heating, and air conditioning. Darkness—another common basement foe—can be overcome by the addition of new lights (the *Sunset* book *Basic Home Wiring Illustrated* tells how).

Depending on your needs, it may not be necessary to improve your entire basement. Instead, consider sectioning off an area with easy access and focus your best efforts there.

All kinds of storage units—closets, cabinets, shelves, and racks—have a place in the basement. You can use masonry fasteners to attach these and other accessories to brick and concrete walls. You may also want to install a combination of such units beneath the stairs.

Even if you don't have a basement, you might have a crawl space between the floor joists and the ground below. There are lots of possibilities—including further excavation—for utilizing this area.

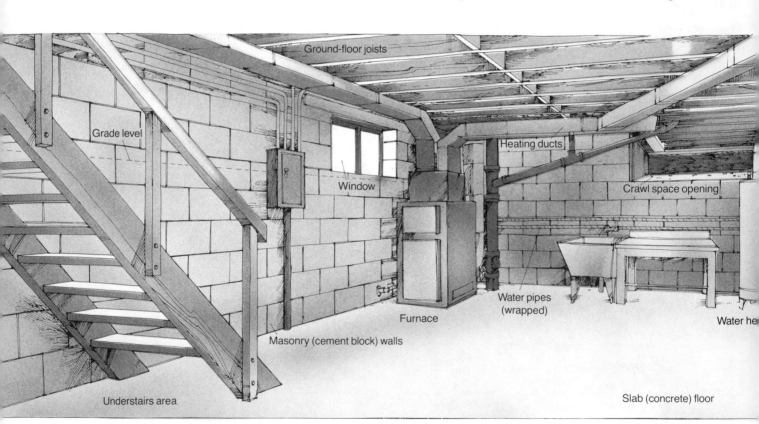

The view down under. *A full basement extends underneath an entire house, and reaches from the slab level to the first floor joists above. Foundation walls—commonly poured concrete or masonry blocks—form the perimeter. Basements are prone to seepage, condensation, and temperature problems, but once these are controlled, basement space is great for storage. Prime storage spots include along the walls, between overhead floor joists, and beneath stairs.*

A basement overview

A basement, loosely defined, is the area between the base of a house's foundation and the floor joists that support the living space above. In the case of a "full" basement, the concrete slab and foundation walls form an enclosed, defined room—but one usually left unimproved by the builders. A full basement has sufficient headroom for a livable space, usually 7½ feet.

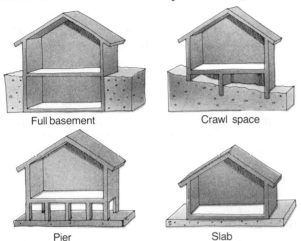

Full basement

Crawl space

Pier

Slab

In many newer homes, the foundation is made shallow to save money and labor, and perhaps to avoid problems with the underground water table. In such cases, only a minimal foundation wall extends above the footings, so basement space is greatly reduced. This kind of mini-basement, or *crawl space,* can still be very useful for storage (see page 79). Split level homes often have both a full basement and crawl space.

Exceptions to the usual basement scheme are pier and slab foundations (see drawing above). Slab foundations are unusable for storage. Pier foundations af-

ford some space, but it's open to the elements, insects, and animals—as well as theft. Hardy storables such as firewood would be fine here; for other types of storage in a pier foundation, use enclosed, lockable units (see "Carport storage ideas," page 66).

Simple basement storage solutions

What kind of storage can you create in your basement without going to very much trouble and expense? If you're lucky enough to have only minor moisture and pest problems, note the precautions that follow.

The structure of your basement may offer ready-to-use storage space: look underneath the stairs, overhead, and around and between ducts. With masonry fasteners you can attach shelves, hooks, and hangers to concrete or brick basement walls.

Moistureproof storage. Waterproofing or dehumidifying may be more expensive than it's worth if the moisture problem is minor and your storage hardy. For damp, unimproved basements, choose metal storage units instead of wood—metal won't swell and warp (though it might rust). Don't pile up containers—let air circulate around them. And don't install closets and cabinets on the floor or against an uninsulated masonry wall; instead, raise them 3 to 4 inches off the ground on a treated wooden base, and fur them out (see page 78) from the wall at least an inch. Heavy polyethylene sheeting placed below and behind storage is an added protection (see drawing below left).

If your basement is subject to occasional flooding or standing water, consider placing loose items on a makeshift raft to float through any unexpected deluge.

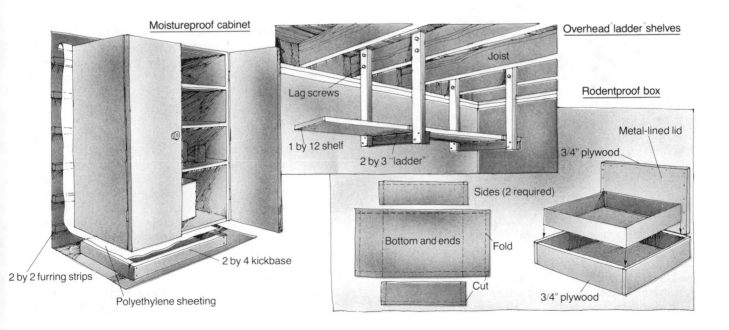

Moistureproof cabinet

Overhead ladder shelves

Joist

Lag screws

Rodentproof box

1 by 12 shelf

2 by 3 "ladder"

Metal-lined lid

3/4" plywood

Sides (2 required)

Bottom and ends

Fold

2 by 2 furring strips

2 by 4 kickbase

Cut

3/4" plywood

Polyethylene sheeting

Rodentproof storage. A basement with a dirt floor is a rat's delight. A good cement wall-and-slab foundation certainly helps keep rats and mice at bay. Most rodents enter through rotted sheathing (just above the foundation wall), dilapidated vent screens, and vent pipes; check these regularly. Metal containers, taped shut, or plywood boxes lined with sheet metal (see drawing on page 75) will keep rodents away from stored items.

Ideas for overhead storage. An unfinished basement is "roofed" with the floor joists and subfloor materials of the rooms above. The spaces between exposed joists, and the clearance between your head and the joists, are excellent for storing small goods. Pick spots that are free of girders, ducts, and wiring.

Nail plywood or boards across several joists to create overhead shelves; two strips in line make a rack. Shelves suspended with rope or chain or "ladder shelves" (see drawing on page 75) are easy to make.

Understairs storage. A frequently wasted space, the wedge-shaped area under stairs offers the space-conscious homeowner a place to build tailored shelves, roll-out bins, cupboards, or a closet. Straight-run stairs offer access from one or both sides; L or U-type stairs may provide several individual cubbyholes.

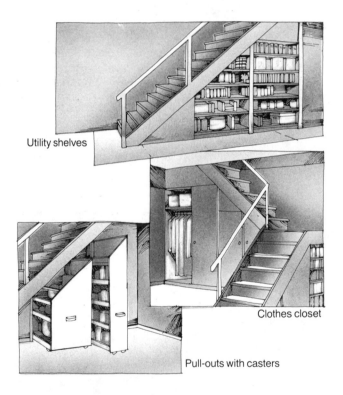

Utility shelves

Clothes closet

Pull-outs with casters

Attaching storage units to walls. If you've solved the moisture problem, basement walls are prime spots for shelving, pegboards, and hanging cabinets (see pages 6–11). It's easy if you have wood stud walls inside the foundation wall, because the units can be attached with standard woodscrews, nails, or lag screws. If you're fastening directly to masonry, see page 79.

Dealing with moisture and temperature

Here's a game plan for beating moisture buildup and temperature fluctuations, the major opponents of basement storage.

Moisture buildup

Correct diagnosis is the key to solving basement moisture problems, which range from the subtle drip of condensation to a running stream. Where does the water come from and how does it get in?

Most basement moisture problems are the result of improper drainage away from the house and foundation. When water builds up near the foundation, hydrostatic pressure eventually drives it to seep through or actually crack masonry walls or floors. Your best course of action is to prevent moisture buildup at the source. These are the most common culprits:
- *Clogged gutters* that concentrate water and cause overflow near the house walls.
- *Downspouts* that aren't connected to drainpipes or tiles to lead water away from the house.
- *Improper grading*—less than 1 inch of drop for each of the first 10 feet away from the house.
- *Flowerbeds* that pool and store water.
- *Window wells* around basement windows that lack drainage or proper caulking or weatherstripping.

· If you can actually *see* water leaking through your basement wall, you'll probably have to stem the flow of water at its source; see the preceding list and the drawing above right for pointers. The alternative is waterproofing the wall itself from the outside—a messy and costly job.

A serious flow of moisture can't simply be plugged up from inside the basement, but many minor ones can. Here's how:

Stopping seepage. Masonry sealers, primarily of Portland cement, chemical combinations, or both, are designed to stop seepage. Follow the manufacturer's instructions closely; most require a clean wall and two coats. The powder types, less convenient than the liquids, can be applied to a wet wall—which is, alas, often what you'll have to work with.

Stopping minor leaks. Common sites of leaks are between masonry blocks, in stress cracks, and where the foundation wall meets the floor slab. Portland cement—or heavy-duty patching mixtures containing Portland cement—can be pressed into a crack after it's been enlarged with a cold chisel. Again, follow the instructions provided by the manufacturer. Some compounds are formulated for use on active leaks.

Condensation occurs when humid interior air meets a colder surface—an outside wall or cold-water pipe. Sweating pipes are one tipoff; wrap them with insulating tape or special jackets and a vapor barrier. To test

Stopping the flow. *Basement water buildup can usually be traced to familiar outside problems.*

Be sure that gutters are adequate and in good condition. Downspout flow should be steered at least 10 feet from the house to drain or dry properly; provide drainage for window wells, too.

Flowerbeds that pool water next to the house should be moved, or at least sloped for a distance of 6 to 8 feet to hasten runoff; for proper grading in general, provide a drop of at least 1 inch for each of the first 10 feet away from the house.

Clogged gutter

Downspout flow

Window well

Flowerbeds

Improper grading

whether your problem is condensation or seepage, tightly tape a square of thin metal or aluminum foil to the foundation wall, and leave it for a few days. If moisture builds up on the wall side of the foil, it's seepage; on the basement side, condensation.

Insulating basement walls (page 78) will eliminate most condensation problems. Even opening a window helps. If the problem persists, the answer is often an electric dehumidifier. To be effective, a dehumidifier usually requires an air temperature of at least 60°.

The water table blues. At some level below the ground lurks the water table. Its depth varies with the topography, season, and soil, among other factors. An excavated basement may suddenly "fall" below the water table after a heavy rain, causing floor seepage or actual flooding. To find out if you're getting seepage from below, tape a small square of plastic to the basement floor. If the floor beneath the plastic is wet after a few days, seepage is occurring.

Water table problems are difficult to remedy. If the problem is slight, you can waterproof the floor and build a new floor above it (see pages 78–79), or simply elevate your storage units. If the problem is more severe, either embed perforated drain pipe around the perimeter of the floor (a laborious project) or install an automatic sump pump to at least handle flooding.

Temperature: the ups and downs

Ideally, most of your basement should be warm and dry, but you may want to plan some cooler space for a wine cellar—and if you're a gardener, you may be wishing for cool and even humid storage for root crops. Wall off a separate, insulated area—large or

small—adjacent to an outside wall for your cold storage. Then heat the remaining basement space.

Cooling. Basically, you have two cooling options: natural and mechanical. Natural cooling takes advantage of outside air and ground temperatures to cool the air, and an insulated space to maintain the coolness. Construct a simple room on the basement's north or east side; insulate the new inside walls (see page 78 for tips on building and insulating walls) and the ceiling above the room to confine the cold air and to prevent warm air from entering. Vent the space to the outside (see food storage on pages 26–27, for details). A natural cooling system might involve a manually controlled vent with a thermostat you must regulate.

For food or wine storage, you may need a more reliable mechanical cooling system. Mechanical units include thermostat-controlled vent fans, window air conditioners, or even an old refrigerator (its door removed) recessed into an inside wall (otherwise, heat from coils would dilute the cooling effect). If the outside air temperature is above 40° for a significant part of the food storing season, or if you want to create a wine cellar in a climate with temperatures commonly above 60°, investigate mechanical means for cooling your basement.

Heating. Your basement or crawl space may already be heated—at least indirectly—by your house's central heating system. If not, check the system's capacity, and if possible run new ducts to the basement space. If you don't have a central heating system, consider an independent source of heat: a gas, electric, or kerosene heater, portable or built-in. See page 67 for more information.

Basic basement improvements

After you've conquered any moisture problems your basement might have, you can move on to other improvements that will make it weathertight for storage or multipurpose use—like a garage, a basement often doubles as a workshop, crafts studio, or laundry room. You'll find here the basic techniques for insulating and "furring out" masonry walls, and for building a subfloor. For more improvement ideas, see "Garages," especially pages 66–67.

Beefing up basement walls

Two basic ways to build up masonry walls (see drawing below) are with furring strips or standard 2 by 4 framing. Furring strips—2 by 2s or 1 by 3s—are attached directly to masonry walls with paneling adhesive, or with hammer or gun-driven masonry nails (see facing page). Walls built from 2 by 4s "float" in front of masonry walls—or can be positioned anywhere within the basement. They provide a better "dead" space for condensation control, as well as extra room for thicker insulation and for wiring. They are, however, more expensive and complicated to build than furring-strip walls. (See the drawing below for examples of both types.)

Types of insulation commonly used on basement walls include rigid polystyrene boards, fiberglass blankets, and fiberglass batts. If the insulation you choose doesn't include a vapor barrier (pages 70–71), add a complete layer of polyethylene (at least 2 mils thick) over the studs and insulation. Rigid board insulation and the vapor barriers on fiberglass types are flammable and should be covered with ½-inch gypsum wallboard or another fire-retardant material.

The soil itself is a good insulator. It's usually not necessary to insulate more than 2 feet below grade in many areas or below the frost line in others; check with your local building department.

High and dry basement floors

If you can't cure your cold, leaky basement floor, build another one above it (see drawing on facing page).

For the best results in problem cases, first cover the old slab with asphalt. Be sure to plug any floor drains. Floor framing of 1 by 4 sleepers (see drawing on facing page) is attached with masonry nails (see below right) to the slab. Add shims or wood blocks below the sleepers to level out a sloping or wavy floor. If your new floor is to be of plywood sheeting, be sure the sleepers are spaced on 16 or 24-inch centers. Insulation between sleepers is optional—it's not strictly necessary when the slab is below grade.

With the sleepers in place, spread 4-mil polyethylene sheeting (for a vapor barrier) over their tops, overlapping and taping all edges together. Next, add another layer of 1 by 4s above the first, "sandwiching" the sheeting. Then lay your subflooring— plywood or "1-by" floor boards (see page 72).

A simpler flooring job, if your slab is dry and level, entails brushing on a chemical sealer, then laying tiles—asphalt or vinyl-asbestos—directly on the slab.

Masonry fasteners

Fastening storage units, brackets, and structural framing to masonry is a challenge. Fortunately, a good selection of tried-and-true hardware and techniques is available. The composition of the wall or floor you're working with and the type of fixture to be attached determine what kind of fasteners you should use. Some tips: always attach fasteners to solid masonry, not to the mortar between segments; cement block foundations, because of their hollow construction, require toggle bolts or very short plugs; and always wear

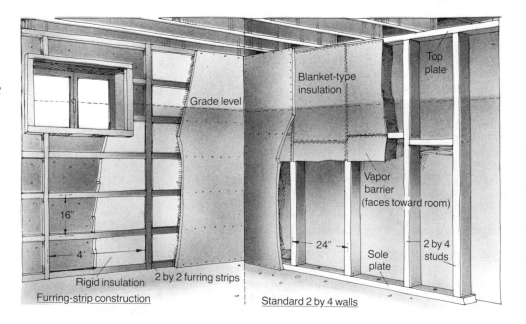

Two types of walls. *Furring-strip construction is less expensive and easier to build than standard 2 by 4 walls. The 2 by 4s provide better condensation control, though, and room for wiring and thicker insulation.*

Grade level

Blanket-type insulation

Top plate

Vapor barrier (faces toward room)

16"

4'

Rigid insulation

2 by 2 furring strips

Furring-strip construction

24"

Sole plate

2 by 4 studs

Standard 2 by 4 walls

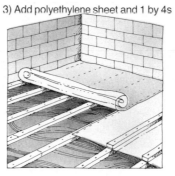

1) Waterproof   2) Lay 1 by 4 sleepers   3) Add polyethylene sheet and 1 by 4s   4) Lay subflooring

Follow these four steps *to build a floor in your basement.*

safety glasses when drilling holes in masonry or driving masonry nails.

Expansion anchors include fiber and plastic plugs, and lead expansion shields and plugs. Use fiber or plastic plugs for lightweight installations, where you'd normally use woodscrews. Expansion shields, which secure lag bolts or machine screws, are for heavy jobs—hanging large shelf units or cabinets from walls, or anchoring the sole plate of a new wall to the floor.

All expansion anchors are installed in a similar manner. Drill a hole the diameter of, and slightly longer than, the plug in the wall or floor. Use either a star drill and hammer, or an electric drill equipped with a carbide-tipped bit. Tap the plug in. Insert the screw or bolt through the fixture to be attached, and drive it into the plug.

Masonry nails. Driven with a hammer or a .22-caliber cartridge-powered stud gun, masonry "cut" nails, pins, and studs are excellent where strength isn't critical, because they're simple to install. Use them for fastening furring strips to a masonry wall and for hanging lightweight brackets and accessories. Stud guns, commonly available for rent, can fire pins through a 2 by 4 sole plate into a concrete floor to anchor a wall.

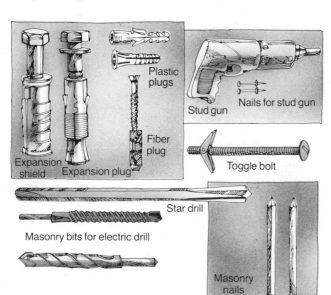

Plastic plugs

Stud gun   Nails for stud gun

Fiber plug

Expansion shield   Expansion plug   Toggle bolt

Star drill

Masonry bits for electric drill

Masonry nails

Toggle bolts. Hollow cement block foundation walls demand toggle bolts. Drill a hole in the wall just large enough for the wings (see drawing) to pass through when compressed. Thread the bolt through the fixture to be mounted, attach the wings, and slip the assembly through the hole. Once through, the wings will spring open, then pull up against the back of the wall when the bolt is tightened.

Crawl space improvements

Though you're desperate for storage space and lack a full basement, if you have a crawl space you may still be in luck. As long as you can negotiate at a crawl and sit up without bonking your head, the space is usable.

If your crawl space is less than 4½ feet deep—or in any case if it inspires feelings of claustrophobia—you'll need to enlarge it by excavating.

Access. If you need to provide entry to your crawl space from above, where is it convenient? An out-of-the-way kitchen pantry or a large hall closet, perhaps? A ladder or a steeply angled ladderlike set of stairs is your best route of descent. The door itself may be a simple trap or a larger double door.

Excavating can be messy as well as awkward, evoking memories of prison escape movies. For cement or asphalt surfaces, you'll need a pick, cement chisel, or jack. Excavate only the area you'll need, which could be as small as 3 feet deep and 5 feet square. Be careful that no water pipes or sewer lines are in the area—look over your house's plans before starting to dig.

If the water table rises above your excavation, you'll end up with a pool of water instead of a storage area. Check with the local building department for underground water levels in your area.

Flooring. A dirt floor can be left as is or covered with new cement, asphalt, sawdust, wood chips, pebbles, or plastic sheeting. A cement floor is framed with a wooden form, then poured using a shovel and wheelbarrow from above or inside (see the *Sunset* book *Basic Masonry Illustrated* for more detailed information). You can insert anchor bolts for stud frame walls in the cement while it's wet.

INDEX